The Robert E. Howard Guide

THE ROBERT E. HOWARD GUIDE

Patrice Louinet

2018

For Glenn Lord and Rusty Burke.
Mentors, gentlemen, friends.

Table of Contents

List of Plates

Acknowledgements

Special thanks to Barbara Barrett, Paul Herman, Jeffrey Shanks, Rob Roehm, Leonidas Vesperini, Jérôme Vincent, Todd Vick, and Barnabidule.

Introduction

The American edition of *The Robert E. Howard Guide* follows the French one by more than two years, a rather uncommon occurrence, as it is usually the other way around. Howard's popularity is at an all-time high in the latter country, but several indicators show that a similar movement is at work in the United States (and elsewhere in the world for that matter). Whichever side of the Atlantic you live on, this upsurge owes little to coincidence and is instead the logical extension of a movement that began at the turn of the new millennium, when the Conan stories—a cornerstone of modern fantasy—were published in an unexpurgated and untampered-with edition for the first time ever.

In the wake of this milestone edition, an impressive portion of Howard's fiction has been published or reprinted under the guidance of the leading Howard scholars, systematically using the purest texts available. At the same time, serious investigation of Howard's life, influences and achievements put to rest most of the distortions and manipulations that were introduced by the very same people who had been in charge of the promotion of the Conan stories, Howard's most famous creation by far. While citing Howard as an influence was particularly unwise (and rare) twenty years ago, an author like G.R.R. Martin explains nowadays that every lover of fantasy should begin by reading Howard and Tolkien, and numerous up-and-coming authors now casually name-drop Howard as an influence.

This book has thus become a necessity for the simple reason that Robert E. Howard, his works, and his importance in the fantasy genre is being entirely reevaluated. The brisk sales of the Del Rey Conan volumes beginning in the early years of the millennium soon led to a series of comic-book adaptations by Dark Horse, but it has only been in the last couple of years that the impact of these restored editions has started to make itself felt, when a major tabletop board game and a role playing game entered production. Both adaptations have remained as close as possible to the source material, i.e. to Howard, a huge and welcome change from previous adaptations. At the other end of the spectrum, academia is starting to pay attention to Howard, something which simply wasn't possible when there was no standard textual edition available. Howard has become a staple at the Popular Culture Association (PCA) conference and the International Conference for the Fantastic in the Arts (ICFA) in the United States, and is/has been the subject of several PhD dissertations worldwide, and notably in prestigious universities in Japan, Canada, Switzerland, and France, the latter at the prestigious Sorbonne.

In spite of this increased notoriety, though, the fact remains that for the public at large, Howard is still an unknown and Conan is more often than not reduced to Arnold Schwarzenegger, the muscular political opinions of John Milius, Frank Frazetta's paintings, or the barbarian in a fur-diaper popularized by Marvel Comics in the 1970s.

The present volume falls within this pivotal new movement. It is first and foremost a guide, which aims at presenting the man and his works in a concise, straightforward and hopefully interesting way, but it is also a manifesto and a watchdog. Its purpose is to dispel—once and for all—the errors, lies, and misconceptions that have been repeated ad nauseam. It should also be useful for the Howard fan in need of an efficient tool to set the record straight.

It is thus militant in places and can be ferocious when needed (we are discussing Howard, after all, so no real surprise here). It is also an account of what has happened and of what is taking place right now. It pays special attention to Conan the Cimmerian, because the character has a tremendous importance in the history of fantasy, in Howard's career, but also, and more importantly, because several of the Conan stories are among the best Howard ever penned. That being said, don't imagine for an instant that you'll find within these pages yet another "Conan biography" or even a chronology. Or even Solomon Kane's timeline. Howard is the subject of this volume, not his various creations. By the same token, you are not going to find a detailed index of the various Conan magazines published by Marvel and Dark Horse over the years. (And in case this was what you wanted, read on. Maybe you won't care so much after you have reached the last page.)

If you don't know anything about Howard beyond his name, you can skip the first part of this book (which deals with the misconceptions surrounding Howard) and get back to this section later. If, on the contrary, you have "read that Howard probably..." a close reading of that chapter will probably be an eye-opening experience. But don't take my word for it. Go read it.

And whether you discovered Howard via Conan, or Conan via Howard, or any other way, let's wager that this guide will show you that the pen can be, at times, as mighty as the sword…

"Fool that I was to trust a Frenchman." – Solomon Kane

Chapter One

Common Misconceptions about Howard

1. Howard was convinced that Conan had really existed.

Even if he was not at the origin of this (in)famous assertion, John Milius, director of the 1982 *Conan the Barbarian* movie, is responsible for its popularity. The filmmaker repeated the anecdote on several occasions, most noteworthily in "Conan Unchained," a documentary about the making of the movie, in which he declares: "[Howard] was convinced that, you know, the town wanted to exterminate him, this kind of thing, and he'd go home and board up his windows and load rifles—complete nut! But the best part is, he's alone one night, and he feels a shadow overtake him from behind, and he knows that Conan is standing behind him with a large axe. And Conan tells him, 'Just stay there and write, and if you don't do exactly what I'm gonna tell you, I'm gonna cleave you down the middle.' And so, he's so terrified, because Conan just exudes such power and fear, and he could just see the axe glinting in his peripheral vision, you know, that he just writes all night!"

Research has failed to unearth any letter, document or interview in which we learn that the whole town wanted to exterminate Howard, or that he would board up his windows and load rifles. These are pure Milius inventions. The Conan episode is based on a passage from a Howard letter, but distorted almost beyond recognition. On 14 December 1933, Howard wrote Clark Ashton Smith:

"I know that for months I had been absolutely barren of ideas, completely unable to work up anything sellable. Then the man Conan seemed suddenly to grow up in my mind without much labor on my part and immediately a stream of stories flowed off my pen—or rather, off my typewriter—almost without effort on my part. I did not seem to be creating, but rather relating events that had occurred. Episode

Robert E. Howard

crowded on episode so fast that I could scarcely keep up with them. For weeks I did nothing but write of the adventures of Conan. The character took complete possession of my mind and crowded out everything else in the way of story-writing. When I deliberately tried to write something else, I couldn't do it. I do not attempt to explain this by esoteric or occult means, but the facts remain. I still write of Conan more powerfully and with more understanding than any of my other characters; but the time will probably come when I will suddenly find myself unable to write convincingly of him at all. That has happened in the past with nearly all my rather numerous characters; suddenly I would find myself out of contact with the conception, as if the man himself had been standing at my shoulder directing my efforts, and had suddenly turned and gone away, leaving me to search for another character."

What this tells us is that Howard was, first and foremost, a storyteller; a man who would never let the factual truth stand between him and a good story. If we are to believe his correspondence, he only needed to sit down at his typewriter, and the stories would almost write themselves. The truth is more prosaic. In most cases, and increasingly as the years went by, Howard spent time working on and polishing his texts. Several drafts were usually needed before he was satisfied with a story. In those pre-word processor days, he would often rewrite a whole page because he was unhappy with a sentence or two. But he would almost systematically lead his correspondents to believe that writing was a "natural" activity for him. The two-thousand three-hundred pages of Conan drafts that have come to us attest to the seriousness with which Howard plied his trade. Howard had used the exact same argument when discussing the Kull stories with H.P. Lovecraft, explaining that the "three stories I wrote about that character seemed almost to write themselves, without any planning on my part; there was no conscious effort on my part to work them up. They simply grew up, unsummoned, full grown in my mind and flowed out on paper from my fingertips." Howard was simply "forgetting" the ten other tales in the series, aborted or rejected. If the Texan used the imagery of the Cimmerian standing at his back to help him write, it was no more than that: a mere image. That Howard felt the need of a "connection" with his characters to write more powerfully and with more conviction there is no doubt. That Howard feared Conan's axe was just Milius selling the idea of a crazy Howard.

2. Howard killed himself because he couldn't face life without his mother.

When Howard learned on the morning of June 11, 1936 that his mother had just sunk into an irreversible coma, he went to his car, parked along the pathway next to the Howard house, and put a bullet in his brain. He thus didn't commit suicide when he heard that his mother had died, but after he was informed that she would never regain consciousness. Hester Jane Howard had been ailing for several months, and her impending death had been in evidence since the beginning of 1936. Howard had been haunted by suicide for many years, well before his mother's health started deteriorating. In 1923, aged 17, he was apparently quite troubled when a classmate killed himself. His close friend Frank Thurston Torbett explained that when Howard was "blue and depressed" he would talk about suicide and how he thought of committing it. In a July 1925 letter, Howard writes, on the wake of a painful incident: "I really never expected to leave that office when I entered it, alive. I sat and the night passed and cold sweat stood upon my forehead as I fought out my silent battle." It is difficult to determine if Howard was sincere or being overly melodramatic here. In a 1932 missive, he states: "By the way, there's something I've been intending to speak to you about for some time; in the event of my death, I wish you'd drop a line to each of the following [people]..." Howard's father, Isaac Mordecai Howard, never accepted the idea that his son had had suicidal tendencies and/or obsessions for a long time. He attempted to cover up elements after the suicide, trying to make it appear that his son's act was simply the consequence of his despondency over his mother's death—a tragedy that corresponded to a very peculiar state of mind and was in no way representative of his son's temperament; a happy family torn apart by a tragic incident. The inscription on the family's gravestone is quite eloquent: "They were lovely and pleasant in their life, and in their death they were not divided" (2 Samuel 1:23). Thus, when Isaac Howard found "The Tempter," a poem glorifying suicide, in his son's papers, he had it published in The Cross Plains Review, the hometown paper, on the occasion of the first anniversary of his son's death, explaining that "the poem was written only forty-eight hours before the youthful literary genius fired a fatal bullet through his brain." The close study of a draft of the poem shows without the shadow of a doubt that this

Hester Howard and Robert's dog Patch

poem dates at the latest from 1929, seven years before. Isaac Howard couldn't know that, but he also couldn't know that it had been typed "48 hours" before the suicide. That Howard was close to his mother is indisputable, but her death was obviously not the cause of his suicide. It simply *provided the occasion* Howard had been waiting for. At the moment he learned, not that she was dead, but that she no longer needed him to look after her, Howard found himself master of his fate again, and in a position to do what he had been considering for months at the very minimum, and probably for years.

3. Conan enjoyed a special status in Howard's mind.

No one can deny that Howard earned his literary fame and posterity thanks to Conan of Cimmeria. However, one should not infer that the character enjoyed the privileged status most people would like to assign him, i.e. that Conan was his "ultimate" creation, the one he would keep writing about, story after story, year after year.

From a strictly commercial viewpoint, the eighteen Conan stories pale against the thirty-seven tales devoted to Steve Costigan, the boxing mariner of the *Sea-Girl*, and the twenty-one yarns devoted to Breckinridge Elkins of Bear Creek. Howard was in the habit of going from one character to the next. Sometimes, after several unfruitful attempts he would suddenly realize he was unable to write convincingly about this character anymore, as explained above. In rare instances, he would go back to a character after several months, or even a year, but this was the exception rather than the rule. In that respect, Conan was no different from the Texan's numerous other creations. He wrote the last Conan story—"Red Nails"—in July 1935, eleven months before his death. The year before, he had confided Novalyne Price that he was "getting a little tired of Conan," that he had other aspirations and wanted to devote his time to more ambitious tales, and especially write about the history of the American Southwest. It could of course be argued that the two Conan stories composed at about the time he was making these declarations, tales that almost every critic ranks as the best in the series: "Beyond the Black River" and "Red Nails," are exactly that: "serious" (Conan) stories set in (a Hyborian version of) the American West, dealing with quintessential Western themes.

On the other hand, it has been noted that, when Howard launched a new series, the first tales were usually much more original and captivating than those that would follow (perhaps for the reasons delineated above). The Conan tales, however, don't follow that rule: they are characterized by a high level of quality throughout, except for a five month period in late 1932-early 1933, when Howard, suddenly confronted by a particularly difficult financial situation, found himself forced to make money as quickly as possible and thus wrote Conan tales he knew would sell immediately (and slanted to grab the cover illustration). It didn't take Howard long to realize that Conan could become an almost instant cash-machine, a "meal-ticket," as he would have it some time later. Once back on his financial feet, Howard resumed writing more ambitious or experimental Conan stories again, and even started playing with the codes he had himself created a couple of years earlier with "The Phoenix on the Sword."

Lastly, it could be posited that Howard ceased writing Conan stories *only* because *Weird Tales*, the pulp magazine in which the stories appeared, was chronically late in its payments (sometimes more than a year after publication) due to being on very shaky financial grounds. The conventional wisdom is that, had *Weird Tales* paid well and on time, Howard would have kept on writing tale after tale featuring the Cimmerian. But he could have offered the character—or a clone thereof—to another magazine. He had done that in the past when Street & Smith had asked for Steve Costigan, his prize-fighting sailor. Since *Fight Stories* wanted to keep Costigan, Howard had created a new series starring a similar character for the competition. It also happened later, when Howard created not one, but two clones of his best-selling character Breckinridge Elkins. But he did no such thing with Conan, as if he was simply outgrowing his interest in fantasy. A month before his death, Howard wrote: "I find it more and more difficult to write anything but western yarns.... If I can get a series running in *Argosy*, keep the Elkins series running in *Action Stories*, now a monthly, and the Buckner J. Grimes yarns in *Cowboy Stories*, I'll feel justified in devoting practically all my time to the writing of western stories. I have always felt that if I ever accomplished anything worthwhile in the literary field, it would be with stories dealing of the central and western frontier."

Everything thus compels us to believe that the Cimmerian was just one of many characters in Howard's career, a special one indeed, but one who had become, in 1936, a creation belonging to Howard's literary past. Exactly as "had happened in the past with all of [his] rather numerous creations."

4. Howard had a wretched childhood.

It was Lyon Sprague de Camp, at the time editor of the Conan stories (as published by Lancer and then Ace Books), and Howard's first biographer, who created and popularized the idea of Robert E. Howard's hellish early years: a frail boy, sick most of the time, constantly bullied at school and running back home to find solace and protection with his mother. In fact, this is the pillar on which *Dark Valley Destiny* (1983), the biography L. and Catherine Crook de Camp devoted to Howard, is built. The book was an impressive sabotage operation designed to depict Howard as a maladjusted and flawed individual, thus justifying the need for a capable editor to take the reins of the Conan series. That the said editor was de Camp himself was pure coincidence, of course! Scholarly research of the last three decades has shown that the conclusions reached by the de Camps were not only erroneous (which happens to everyone), but that facts were often distorted, and sometimes made up (when they couldn't find elements that backed up their preconceived theories). Howard was thus a "frail and sickly" child... only in the questions the de Camps asked their interviewees. They kept asking for confirmation that Howard was a sickly baby and child. What should have been, at best, a working hypothesis, was hammered as an assertion. (The de Camps needed a wretched childhood to explain the closeness between mother and son that would lead to an Oedipal attachment that would in turn explain Howard's suicide.) However, none of their interviewees could recall the sickly youth the de Camps described. Kate Merryman, who took extensive care of Hester Jane Howard during her final months, a woman Mrs. Howard talked to at length, was one of the two prime informants of the de Camps concerning Howard's first years. Ms. Merryman repeatedly told the de Camps that she had never heard Mrs. Howard say that her son had been sickly and frail. In the published version, the de Camps have Ms. Merryman say that Howard was a sickly child, and the footnote refers the reader to an interview in which she says exactly the opposite. (The fabrication was discovered only a few years ago, when the de Camps' papers were made available to researchers.)

The exact same scenario is repeated when the de Camps discuss Howard's early childhood: "Frail, introverted, and looking to his mother for protection, Robert was a natural butt for bullies. Even before the opening of school, every day saw a series of terrifying encounters, which varied from the merely mean to the Inquisitorial. He could not leave his yard for fear of being set upon." The first problem in that paragraph is that it is based on nothing: no interviewee, letter, or document of any kind hints at anything remotely close to that. The "terrifying encounters" were entirely made up by the de Camps, who conceded that much about Howard's early life had to be "reconstructed." As to Howard's being bullied at school when he was a very small child, it never happened. The last doubts were lifted a few years ago when it was discovered that Howard didn't begin school until 1914, aged eight, not because he was "frightened" or that "leaving his mother's apron" had been a horrifying experience, but

A teenage Howard demonstrating his fighting form.

because school started when you were eight years old in Bagwell, Texas, where the Howards lived at the time. And while we have no real information as to what happened at the Bagwell school, we know it didn't last long: a few weeks later, in January 1915, the Howard family moved to Cross Cut, Brown County. From this period onward, we have the testimonies of several witnesses. Howard had become an avid reader, but he also loved to play with his friends, and was almost systematically described as the one who wrote the scenarios of all their games. So, a few unpleasant experiences in his pre-teen years, some sarcastic remarks because he developed a taste for reading in a region where this was rather uncommon? Maybe. Even probably. A frail and sickly toddler whose childhood was an endless series of nightmares? A pure invention of the de Camps.

5. Howard was a recluse.

Howard spent a good deal of time at home, because he was a writer, probably the most sedentary profession in the world, which is probably responsible for the mental image of a Howard chained to his house. Actually, Howard did travel a lot, covering large distances in his home state of Texas, the size of which has to be factored in. When H. P. Lovecraft, for instance, would go from Providence to Quebec, he was covering fewer miles than Howard did during many of his jaunts within the Lone Star State. When we add his sojourns in New Orleans, New Mexico, Oklahoma, Missouri and Arkansas, we have to conclude that Howard traveled more than many of his contemporaries, especially those living in the same region as him. Furthermore, the Howard family had lived in many areas of Texas before settling in Callahan County.

Far from being a recluse, Howard loved to travel. While he had to work at home and, during the last few years of his life, be present to help take care of his sick mother, his trips became at the same time more numerous and more ambitious as soon as he was in a position to buy his own car. He relished describing his three-day or week-long expeditions in his letters to Lovecraft or August Derleth, covering an impressive number of miles in only a couple of days. Far from being a hindrance, his profession gave him a freedom few have: to work when he wanted to, and take holidays or extended weekends whenever he felt like it (and could afford it, of course). Howard had no boss, no nine-to-five routine and he was the only one to decide how much he wanted to earn. Novalyne Price, whom he dated in the mid-1930s, explained that he particularly liked to have conversations with the locals and old-timers of the localities they were visiting. He loved to hear the stories and the legends of the old west, of the antebellum days, of the Indian wars, etc. Such journeys and encounters furnished him with many an idea and background material for his latter tales. His visit to the Carlsbad caverns, for instance, inspired the background of a Conan tale, and we'll see later how his impression of Lincoln, New Mexico, where the famous Bloody Lincoln County War had taken place, played a crucial role in the genesis of his Conan masterpiece "Red Nails."

6. Howard made more money than the banker of the town.

Anyone who has read more than a few paragraphs about Howard can't have missed a reference to Howard described as a successful writer, with the inevitable remark that he made more money than the town's banker did. What we know for sure is that Howard's earnings rose rapidly between 1927 and 1928, when he made writing his profession in earnest, and that the numbers remained fairly high until 1931. In 1932, the recession dealt a severe blow to his income as several pulps he was selling to went out of business, depriving him of sources of regular and semi-regular income: *Fight Stories* and *Action Stories*, in which appeared his humorous boxing stories, and *Strange Tales of Mystery and Terror*, a fairly recent but promising market, direct competitor to *Weird Tales*. Income for 1932 and early 1933 was down, but began taking an impressive turn for the better in late 1933, a few months after Howard had hired an agent on a non-exclusive basis. 1934 was an exceptional year, topped only by 1936, even though Howard died in June of the latter. In the weeks preceding his death, he had—at long last—succeeded in getting published in the prestigious *Argosy* with a promise of regular sales, had an agent who was firmly convinced of his promising future, and he was repeatedly trying to crash the British market, which he would do, albeit posthumously, with the sale of the novel *A Gent from Bear Creek* in late 1936. We have a fairly good idea of how much money Howard earned from the sales of his stories for every year of his life, though a few numbers are not known exactly. Even though *Weird Tales*, the pulp magazine he had built his career on, was chronically late and owed him over $1,300 at the time of his death, everything shows that Howard earned much, much more than the average inhabitant of his hometown of Cross Plains. Norris Chambers, born in 1918 and a young man when Howard died, would later explain that most of the small town's inhabitants earned anywhere between three and eight hundred dollars a year in those times. Howard was way above that every year of his professional life.

On the other hand, we don't know how much the "banker" earned. The two banks of the town closed in 1931, with one reopening a few months later under a new name, but it is unlikely the president was a local. The "banker" alluded to was probably the person in charge of the local branch. We have no idea who he was, and thus of how much he earned. Or even if there was only one banker. The source of the anecdote has never been traced.

> *"Robert Howard found a purse on the streets last week containing fifty dollars, and he immediately set out to find the owner. C. D. Henson of Cross Cut was the man, and he soon had the purse and the money. That's honesty as we define it."* The Cross Plains Review, *23 December 1927*

7. Robert E. Howard died a virgin.

The question of Howard and his relations with women in general has long been muddled because of, once again, the biographical writings of L. Sprague de Camp, who promoted the idea of a Howard afflicted with a textbook case of the Oedipus complex pathology. As a consequence, the young Texan could only be eminently chaste, shy to the extreme with women, and thus died before experiencing the "little death."

As he was undergoing a medical check-up in 1930, Howard explained to the physician that he had felt his first sexual impulses when aged "19 or 20." Those awakening interests interestingly—and logically—found their way into his writings beginning in 1925 (when Howard was 19) with "Wolfshead," an unbridled fantasy adventure, certain episodes of which seem to echo Howard's recent and clumsy attempts at seducing the rather "fast" woman one of his best friends was dating at the time. Howard had long been professing that he had no interest in dating girls, maybe because of an excessive teenage shyness or due to a (too) chivalric (to be honest) temperament. Some have even ventured to see in the chaste Kull of Atlantis (created 1926-1927) a projection of Howard himself, but just as romantic

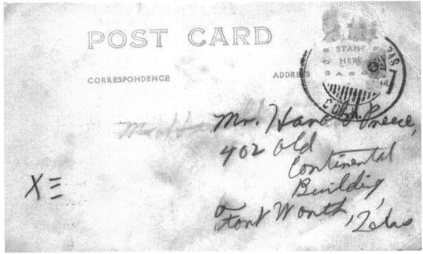

Postcard from Howard to his friend Harold Preece showing the customs house at Piedras Negras, a Mexican border town known for its legal brothels.

interests started to become a staple of the Kull stories by 1928, Howard's shifting interests are obvious to anyone who has read his letters from that period. It is thus more than probable that tourism wasn't Howard's main preoccupation when he spent a few days in Mexico in the early part of June 1928, and especially in Piedras Negras, the border town then favored by a good many young American males, at a time when it was common practice to discover sexuality with a hired

30

professional. Of course, no one would ever write of the actual experience, but Howard made no mystery of what the town had to offer in terms of pleasures in a letter to Clyde Smith. In the weeks that followed, Howard's letters became replete with poems and texts that ranged from the bawdy to the erotic, and even, for some entries, the pornographic. If it is impossible to determine whether this should be interpreted as a "pronounced interest" or the result of the discovery of sex, it can't be denied that the 1928 Howard had very little in common with his younger self in that respect.

At the end of that year, Howard shocked his intellectual friends when he announced that he was very interested in a young girl he nicknamed the "diabolical blond." The episode, as recounted by de Camp, is infinitely chaste: Howard, having fallen in love, enrolled at Sunday school so he could see the girl of his dreams fairly regularly and, maybe, reveal his flame. Fifty years after the fact, when de Camp interviewed Ruth Baum, supposedly the woman in question, it was her turn to be surprised: she had never noticed that Howard was interested in her. de Camp's conclusion was evident: Howard was so shy with her (read: with women in general) that she hadn't even realized he was attracted to her. There were three slight problems with that conclusion: Ruth Baum was already married in 1928, she was a brunette, and she lived in Brownwood, not Cross Plains. The only reason she had never noticed anything was simply because Howard had no romantic interest whatsoever in her, a fact de Camp either hadn't seen or hadn't wished to see. Howard's intentions toward the "diabolical blond," whoever she was, were much less prudish than what we had been led to believe.

Howard had one serious relationship in his life, with Novalyne Price, whom he dated from August 1934 to mid-1935, followed by a strained period of awkward relations, and which was the basis for *One Who Walked Alone*, Novalyne's 1986 memoir written from the diary she kept in those years. Her husband William was still alive at the time, which may explain why the book doesn't elaborate on the more intimate moments she and Bob had. She would later admit that Howard was a very good kisser, for instance. The relationship was serious enough that both of them had thoughts of marriage, albeit never at the same time.

Howard and women? The short answer is that all of the evidence indicates that Bob Howard was nothing more, nothing less, than a man of his times.

> *In 1926, the artist in charge of drawing the cover of* Weird Tales *illustrating "Wolfshead" misplaced the typescript that he was using as reference material. Editor-in-chief Farnsworth Wright immediately asked Howard to send his carbon copy, if handy, so that the story could be typeset. Howard, far from being an accomplished professional at the time, had made no carbon. (He would, almost systematically, after this incident). He offered to rewrite the story from "his notes" (i.e. his memory) and did so. The original typescript was eventually located (minus the first page) and "Wolfshead" was cover-featured on the April 1926 issue. Lucky for Howard that he had an eidetic memory. A friend recalled how he was able to recite Coleridge's "Rhyme of the Ancient Mariner" after having read it only twice.*

8. Howard was sympathetic toward fascism.

It would be difficult to find something Howard hated more than fascism. Born and bred in a 1920s and 1930s semi-rural Texas severely hit by the Great Depression, Howard was wary of every form of organized system, and fascism was no exception to the rule. He repeated it over and over in his correspondence with H.P. Lovecraft, whose views on the matter were quite divergent, to wit this passage from Howard's December 1934 missive: "You accuse me of 'hating human development' because I mistrust Fascism.... But you can not prove that Fascism is anything but a sordid, retrogressive despotism, which crushes the individual liberty and strangles the intellectual life of every country it inflicts with its slimy presence." It would be difficult to be more to the point.

Not that it means Howard wasn't a racist. He was, like most of his contemporaries, guilty of that everyday, casual racism (some would say racialism) that was prevalent then, especially so in rural and semi-rural areas, expressing views that were unfortunately all too common. Compared to most of his fellow citizens, he was certainly more progressive (unable to understand, for example, a local law that prevented a "colored person" visiting the area to spend the night in the county). But it remains that several passages in his correspondence and in some stories are devoid of any ambiguity as to the openly racist views of their author.

What is striking in the case of Howard, though, is how his ideas on the question evolved. They didn't change because he found himself increasingly in contact with people of a different country, creed or color—there was simply no such diversity in Cross Plains— but because of the implications of his political and philosophical stances. Confronted with the erudition of Lovecraft, Howard slowly articulated his own philosophical positions, citing individual liberty as the first and most important of principles, before any economic, patriotic or even racial considerations. Without trying to whitewash Howard and exonerate him, one will have a good idea of his political and moral leanings toward the end of his life with the following extract, which needs some contextualizing: In 1935, as they were still arguing the merits of barbarism vs. civilization in their three-year long debate on the subject, Lovecraft professed his admiration for fascism and Mussolini. Howard's reply was a particularly scathing one:

"You express amazement at my statement that 'civilized' men try to justify their looting, butchering and plundering by claiming that these things are done in the interests of art, progress and culture. That this simple statement of fact should cause surprise, amazes me in return. People claiming to possess a superior civilization have always veneered their rapaciousness by such claims. You say some wars are waged in defense of civilization. Can you name a recent one? Was it the Mexican War in which a Latin culture was simply replaced, in some regions, by an Anglo-Saxon culture? Was it the Civil War, in which an agricultural oligarchy was crushed by an industrial oligarchy? Was it the Spanish-American War in which our capitalists grabbed an island for its wealth in sugar? Or was it the world war in which the Germans butchered to expand Kultur, and the Allies fought 'to make the world safe for democracy'? (and incidentally to protect Wall Street's European investments.) Or is it the present tussle in Africa where the wops are civilizing the benighted Ethiopians with poison gas and dum-dum bullets?

"I find it hard to understand your surprise because I say that civilized men always claim the highest motives, even when perpetrating the most infamous atrocities... Your friend Mussolini is a striking modern-day example. In that speech of his I heard translated he spoke feelingly of the expansion of civilization. From time to time he has announced: 'The sword and civilization go hand in hand!' 'Wherever the Italian flag waves it will be as a symbol of civilization!' 'Africa must be brought into civilization!' It is not, of course, because of any selfish motive that he has invaded a helpless country, bombing, burning and gassing both combatants and non-combatants by the thousands. Oh, no, according to his own assertions it is all in the interest of art, culture and progress, just as the German war-lords were determined to confer the advantages of Teutonic Kultur on a benighted world, by fire and lead and steel. Civilized nations never, never have any selfish motives for butchering, raping and looting; only horrid barbarians have those. When the Belgians mutilated several thousand Congo niggers, that was in the defense of civilization, too. When Germany surged across defenseless Belgium that, too, was in defense of civilization, as represented by themselves. But the Allies, too, defended civilization. Each side claimed to be the sole defender of civilization in that carnage. You say that 'the fruits of civilization must be preserved at all costs.' Just who is trying to loot these fruits? The Ethiopians?"

"Otis and Dorse Odom have two negro boys, about 37 years old, at work for them and the boys are good workers and stay strictly in their places and are obedient and polite. There is a prejudice against the negro in Callahan county, but for the life of me I can't see why as long as they conduct themselves properly and stay in a negro's place. We cannot utilize their labor, farm hands are scarce and at a premium. But give the white man the preference, all things considered." (The Cross Plains Review, 05 March 1915)

9. Howard wrote a poem before committing suicide.

All fled, all done; so lift me on the pyre
The feast is over, and the lamps expire.

The above couplet was found on Howard's typewriter a few minutes after his suicide, as Jack Scott, journalist for the *Cross Plains Review* was arriving on the scene. Scott would later indicate that the

Justice of the Peace had asked him what the poem meant, to which Scott had replied: "I think it means he killed himself."

The anecdote was a pretty one, and full of dark romanticism. Too pretty.

The problem is that, of the thirty or so contemporary press articles and about an equal number of surviving letters exchanged by those who were there on that fateful day, not one mentions the suicide note. The first mention in the local press appeared on July 3rd, probably by way of Isaac Mordecai Howard, Howard's father. He had explained in a letter written a few days before that those few lines had been found not in the typewriter, but on a sheet of paper folded and stuck in his son's wallet, found in his pants' back pocket. Isaac Howard added that he was convinced that the couplet had been written just before the suicide, though he had no evidence to back this up.

It had long been thought that the two lines were paraphrased in part from a poem written by Victorian author Ernest Dowson. This was Farnsworth Wright's conviction as soon as he learned of the suicide and of the note. However, research has since shown that it was almost certainly inspired by a couplet from a poem by Viola Garvin, "The House of Caesar." A couplet for a suicide note, or just two lines jotted down hastily on a piece of paper (as Howard would sometimes do) and stuck in his wallet for weeks, or perhaps months?

Howard had left no suicide note... but one had supposedly come to us. Conversely, Howard had very probably left a will... but it was not fated to come to us.

A few days after Howard took his life, his father, Isaac Howard, helped by a woman named Kate Merryman, was busy putting Howard's papers in order. Miss Merryman stumbled upon a holograph will, in which Howard left all his belongings and rights, not to his father, but to his best friend, Lindsey Tyson. Isaac Howard ordered Merryman never to mention the will to anyone, which was never to be seen again. Paul Harrell, the lawyer who handled all the legal papers of the Howard family, knew of the will, though, and as was bound to happen in such a small town, Tyson eventually heard of the story from Harrell, but decided not to act on it, and never mentioned it to Doctor Howard. He had been deeply affected by the suicide of his best friend, the more so since he had been the one who had—unwittingly—loaned Howard the gun he would kill himself with.

"At the age of fifteen, having never seen a writer, a poet, a publisher or a magazine editor, and having only the vaguest ideas of procedure, I began working on the profession I had chosen."

– Robert E. Howard

Chapter Two
Biography

There are 39 known photos of Robert E. Howard. Six were discovered in the past few years, from two different sources.

Robert Ervin Howard was born on January 22, 1906 in Peaster, a small town situated in Parker County, Texas. He was the son of Isaac Mordecai Howard (1871-1944) and Hester Jane Howard, née Ervin (1870-1936).

Hester Jane was the daughter of George W. Ervin, an energetic man who led a colorful life. He was married twice and fathered sixteen children, Hester being the ninth and penultimate child of the first wife. She would never really get to know her biological mother, who died in 1874, when Hester was only four. The Ervin family succeeded, under the impetus and sense of entrepreneurship of G.W. Ervin, to recover from the blow the Secession War had dealt many Southern families. The brothers and sisters of Hester would for the most part become bankers, newspapermen, doctors… people of definite affluence. Hester Jane spent her first thirty-three years visiting with friends and relatives, never working a single day. A lover of literature and especially poetry, she enjoyed the company of equally well-refined people. It was through one of her brothers that she met the man who was to become probably her first serious suitor, William Ezzell, a journalist and newspaper owner. Some time later, as she was spending time in the quite fashionable Mineral Wells, she very unexpectedly fell under the charm of a penniless country doctor: Isaac Mordecai Howard.

The Howard family came from Arkansas, where they had resided until 1885 before moving to Texas and settling in Limestone County. Isaac Mordecai Howard's brothers and sisters prepared to embark on a life of farming, but Isaac had other ambitions. He wanted to become a physician. He sold his share of the family property, probably to fund his initial training. There was at the time no serious legislation as to the practice of medicine in Texas; one was only required to appear before a commission which would decide whether the applicant was qualified enough. The operation was to be repeated every time the physician moved and changed counties. Isaac Howard began practicing in 1899 in two adjacent counties, then went up to North Texas, alternating time in the Lone Star State and the Indian Territories. If Isaac Howard went so far, it was probably because he wanted to be close to his favorite sister, whose husband was serving five years in the penitentiary for having stolen mules.

Isaac Howard's choices are interesting and quite indicative of his character: he would almost always favor small, even minuscule localities, but that showed definite potential: a future railway station, minerals, promising oil booms, new roads, etc. He would adopt that strategy up to the moment he (almost) decided to settle permanently in the Cross Plains area, in 1915.

Hester Jane and Isaac Howard had almost nothing in common, coming from diametrically opposed worlds. Perhaps seduced by the temperament, the sheer energy and the ambition of the man (qualities which were quite close to those of her father, who had died in 1900), Hester Jane Ervin yielded to the advances of Isaac Howard, and they were married on January 12, 1904.

In 1906, a few months after they had made Peaster their home, their only child, Robert, was born. Several weeks later, the family moved once again, to settle a few dozen miles away, in the minuscule place called "Dark Valley" that would make a lasting impression on Robert—or so he would state in later years. Since the Howards left Dark Valley when Robert was barely two, the vivid "memories" he claimed to have of the first months of his life are much more interesting from a psychological than from a biographical viewpoint. In late 1907, Hester Howard had a miscarriage, an episode that Howard would never allude to in any document that has come to us, which is not surprising at all, since he was in the habit of never discussing or even mentioning subjects that were really painful to him. It could also be that he was never aware of the loss, but one can only be struck by the omnipresence of the theme of the "lost" brother or sister in his works and letters.

In the years that followed, the Howards kept moving from one place to another, albeit always in Texas, sometimes staying a few weeks, at best a few months, in their new homes, probably chasing Isaac Howard's next rainbow, with no real success. As was to be expected, the licensing legislation changed in 1907, and it became mandatory for doctors to participate in actual medical training. Isaac Howard had anticipated the change and had enrolled at the Gate City Medical College in September 1904, graduating in May 1905. However, the college was located in Texarkana, far away from Parker County where Isaac Howard lived at the time. A few years later, it was revealed that the Gate City College was a fraud, a diploma factory, with most of its "students" following courses "by mail," and awarded their "degree" for $50. The diplomas were printed in Latin because, as the soon-to-be convicted dean stated, it would "fool 'em; that's why we print 'em in Latin." Given the dates and locations, Isaac Howard was probably among the many doctors who bought their degree. That being said, he never ceased taking postgraduate courses during his career, going sometimes as far as Dallas or New Orleans, was a subscriber to medical literature and was so appreciated by the inhabitants of Cross Plains and its immediate vicinity that they elected him "Citizen of the Year" in 1935. Isaac Howard was a curious man, with a thirst for knowledge. Among his interests other than regular medicine were religion, yoga (quite the fad then), hypnotism and about every form of alternative medicine.

In January 1915, after several months spent in Bagwell, in the northeastern part of the Lone Star State, Isaac Howard moved once again, this time to Cross Cut, Brown County, then to Burkett, Coleman County, in 1917, and eventually to Cross Plains, Callahan County, in 1919. Despite being located in three counties, all three places are actually very close to each other. Isaac Howard, after years of wandering, was settling down. Howard had first attended school in Bagwell (aged eight, which was the age school began there), and he reached the tenth grade in Cross Plains, which was as far as school went in Cross Plains. He thus went to Brownwood, thirty miles away, for his last high school year, graduating in May 1923.

Young Howard was fondly remembered years later by his Cross Cut and Burkett friends. He was the one who always impressed them. He already had a vivid imagination, read a lot, and would be the one

Robert in a childhood portrait ca. 1911.

Robert as a young boy

A teenage Robert (left) with his mother Hester and father Isaac.

who staged all the children's games. The countryside was the perfect place for a young boy to play at make-believe. One such day, the postmistress of Burkett saw the young Howard and the meeting made such a lasting impression on her that she would write about it many years later: "Absorbed in reading we are unaware of any approach until a big black and white dog wearing a collar bounds down from a ledge of rock behind, startling us.... Almost immediately a call 'Come Patches, come Patches' is heard and looking up in direction of the voice we see a lad of about ten years crossing a fence nearby.... His master approaches our position and politely announces, 'I'm Robert Howard, I am sorry if we frightened you. Patches and I are out for our morning stroll. We like to come here where there are big rocks and caves so we can play make believe. Some day I'm going to be an author and write stories about pirates and maybe cannibals. Would you like to read them?'"

Of these first years in the area, two elements are worth noting. The first being the extended sojourn of the Howard family in New Orleans in 1918, on the occasion of one of Isaac's medical courses. New Orleans was already a bustling metropolis of two hundred thousand inhabitants. The experience was a shock for the young Howard, who had always lived in very small communities lost in the deeps of Texas. Enormous, cosmopolitan, New Orleans was also rich in thrilling sensations: the Howards arrived the day following the eighth murder of the Axman, the serial killer who had been terrorizing the town for over a year. Years later, Howard still had fond memories of the Durel sisters, old maids of French origins, at the house of whom he and his parents were staying; of Joe Rizza, a Sicilian immigrant, and his oyster bar; of a disquieting Black-Asian "mulatto"; of exotic and unknown dishes and smells. He had just discovered civilization on a huge scale.

It was at the exact same time that he discovered the opposite in the form of the most elemental "savages": the Picts. Spending some time in a Canal Street library, he found a book dealing with the first ages of Britain, and marveled at those pages dealing with the Pictish tribes, noting, consciously or not, the name of one of those: Brân. An undying fascination for this people was born.

A second episode with a lasting influence occurred in the summer of 1921, when Howard stumbled upon a copy of *Adventure*. The magazine was, with *Argosy*, the most prestigious of the pulps, between the covers of which one could read the stories of all the major writers of the genre: Rafael Sabatini, Harold Lamb, Talbot Mundy, and others. Howard never forgot the moment and reminisced about it years later, with obvious relish. His vocation to become a writer was truly born at that moment, and the young Texan immediately set out to compose his first tales to submit to *Adventure*. His first effort didn't meet with success, as can be surmised. He was but fifteen.

He was not so easily discouraged. During the next few years, he began dozens of stories, the immense majority of which he never completed, visibly written in the spur of the moment and for the sheer joy of writing. Influenced by the swashbuckling, adventure and historical tales he was reading, Howard created his first "heroes": Bran Mak Morn, Frank Gordon (a.k.a. "El Borak"), Steve Allison (the Sonora Kid), Steve Bender, and others. Other writings, more polished and restrained, were published in the high school and college papers of Cross Plains and Brownwood, but of course, these were neither professional nor paying markets.

The friendships Howard developed in his Cross Cut/Burkett/Cross Plains days were, for some of them, lasting ones, but these were the friends he would have a drink or a walk with, watch a football match or box with. Conversely, his Brownwood friends, especially Truett Vinson and Tevis Clyde Smith, harbored literary and/or journalistic aspirations. They soon became his "intellectual" friends, as opposed to those of Cross Plains, relatively speaking.

The first issue of *Weird Tales* hit the stands in March 1923. It was the first magazine to be devoted entirely to stories of the weird, the supernatural and the unusual. Now legendary in its own right, *Weird Tales* was for most of its run a second-string publication, almost always on the verge of cancellation, with chronic financial problems. We know that Howard discovered it quite early, but while it is possible to detect and often trace Howard's borrowings from his readings of *Adventure*, *Argosy* and the classics of adventure fiction, not one of the stories published in the early years of *Weird Tales* seems to have influenced him on any noticeable degree in his own writings. This is not surprising at all since, of the eighty or so juvenile Howard tales and fragments that have come to us, only four contain an element of fantasy or of the weird, two of which being essentially adventure tales including a reincarnation motif.

In the Fall of 1924, Howard sent a tale to Weird Tales. Titled "Spear and Fang," it takes place during prehistoric times and is

The Three Musketeers - Howard (left), Truett Vinson (center), and Tevis Clyde Smith (right).

Howard (left) squared up in a fighting stance with his friend Dave Lee

devoid of any supernatural element or atmosphere. The story pleased new editor Farnsworth Wright, who bought it for $15 (or $16, depending on the source.) Spurred by this first acceptance, an overjoyed Howard jumped on the occasion and deluged *Weird Tales* with new offerings, but it would take him years before he became a regular. Convinced that his career would take off after "Spear and Fang" was published, he was bitterly disillusioned.

Between 1923 and 1927, Howard worked at a series of small jobs, experiences that were as short as they were inconclusive. He enrolled at the Howard Payne Academy in Brownwood with no great desire to graduate. He would recount this phase of his life in a late 1928 thinly disguised (partly-)autobiographical novel patterned after Jack London's *Martin Eden*, portraying himself as an aspiring writer who doesn't really give himself the means to become truly professional. Isaac Howard would have wanted his son to walk in his footsteps, but he doubtless quickly realized that this would not come to pass.

Just after his graduation from Howard Payne in August 1927, Howard made a deal with his parents: they would support him financially for a year, while he tried to become a self-sustaining professional writer. If he failed, he would take a nine-to-five job.

Howard would explain years later that he had chosen his profession—writing—because it offered him more freedom than any other job and allowed him to work when he wanted to, not when someone told him to come to the office. He once said: "Life's not worth living if somebody thinks he's in authority over you." It had been nearly a year since he had written a story when he made that pact with his parents, but the prospects of becoming an accountant must have acted as the most powerful spur.

He sat down, wrote and sold his first story ("The Dream Snake"), then managed to complete a tale he had been working on for months without ever managing to put the final touches on: "The Shadow Kingdom," the first tale featuring Kull of Atlantis, which he sold for a staggering $100. It was a cornerstone in the history of fantasy literature, but Howard had no idea of what he had just accomplished for posterity. He was just trying to make it as a writer to avoid a life he didn't want. A third sale and a series of poems quickly followed "The Shadow Kingdom." It had only taken him a few weeks after the pact to launch his career.

In early 1928, Howard wrote a short story titled "Solomon Kane", which would appear under the title "Red Shadows". In many ways, this story, replete with fantastic elements but taking place in a historical—or quasi-historical—setting, is as important as "The Shadow Kingdom" in the crystallization of modern fantasy. The story broke about every accepted rule of popular and pulp fiction, and it was on those grounds that the editor at *Argosy* rejected the tale. He must have had misgivings of some sorts, because he felt the need to justify the rejection in a long letter, suggesting that Howard change certain aspects of the tale. Howard didn't modify a word and submitted it to *Weird Tales*, which accepted it at once, published it six months later, featuring it on the magazine cover. Only such an off-the-track magazine as *Weird Tales* would have accepted such an atypical story.

Howard's confidence kept growing. The few months that had elapsed since the deal with his parents had apparently been sufficient to keep at bay, forever, the specter of accounting, the dread of an office job and of a boss too big for his britches.

In 1927, he had met Harold Preece, with whom he initiated a correspondence. Preece was an ardent celtophile and a socialist. He was the one who turned Howard's nascent interest in things Celtic, and more especially Gaelic, into a true passion. While everything points to the contrary, Howard began to dream of himself as a man of almost purely Gaelic stock, with "a touch of the Dane." It was as if he was over-exaggerating the importance of the Ervin (maternal) line to the detriment of his purely English patronym. Under this sudden impetus, Howard's fiction soon became replete with blue-eyed, dark-skinned characters, just like the "Black Irish" he now fancied himself descended from. He started adopting the name "Costigan" (with a few variations on the first or last name: Stephen, Steve, Mike, Costovan, etc.) for many of his characters, and sometimes himself. All this while his 1928 letters are full of interrogations and reflections as to his relationship to the world (in the exact same fashion as his character, Kull of Atlantis, who at this time was being confronted by paranoia in "The Shadow Kingdom," the status of reality versus illusion in "The Mirrors of Tuzun Thune," and the relativity of time and space in "The Striking of the Gong"). Howard fully realized the extent of this Celtic influence on his personality on the occasion of a memorable evening spent with friends, among whom was Harold Preece.

It was also in 1928 that Howard started showing a definite interest in the other sex. While his friends had been used to seeing and considering him as a stainless knight, they were shocked to discover a "new" Howard when he announced that he was very much interested in a "diabolical blond." His letters to Clyde Smith became filled with bawdy and erotic poems.

On the professional front, he made his first sale to a market other than *Weird Tales*. A boxing story, sprinkled with a touch of the weird, opened him the pages of *Ghost Stories*, but it was in early 1929 that boxing fiction enabled him to start earning money on a regular (at least semi-regular) basis, with his first sales to *Fight Stories*, a pulp magazine entirely devoted to stories of the ring. Howard had long been a devotee of the sweet science and was an amateur boxer himself. He was familiar with the milieu, its history, and knew the mechanics of a boxing bout from the inside out. Thus, when Fiction House launched *Fight Stories* in mid-1928, Howard submitted story after story, meeting with a string of rejections that didn't discourage him. Eventually, after a long process of trial and error, he found the right formula, in the person of Steve Costigan, sailor and prizefighter. Combining his interests in boxing, adventure and humor, Howard achieved that most elusive goal: creating a character that was successful enough to transform a couple of tales into a regular series, with the (almost) guaranteed income that goes with it.

1928 and the first half of 1929 were years of literary experimentations with about every possible subject, even those where no one would have expected Howard: westerns (in which he had almost no interest at the time), "true" confessions, realistic and even autobiographical fiction, and slices of life. He also wrote an enormous amount of poetry. More than seven hundred poems have come to us, and we know that dozens, maybe hundreds, were lost over the years. Firmly rooted in the traditional Anglo-Saxon school form of poetry, Howard quickly realized that there was no real market for his poems, and especially for his bitter ones. *Weird Tales* did publish some of them, as well as a few amateur and semi-amateur publications.

On May 3, 1929, *The Cross Plains Review* ran this intriguing piece of news: "Dr. I. M. Howard left on Wednesday of this week for Spur, Texas, where he has gone with a view of tentatively locating there for the practice of his profession. If the climate of that locality is more agreeable to his health he may make it a permanent location; otherwise, he announces, he will return to Cross Plains." Spur is a hundred and fifty miles from Cross Plains. The reasons for this move remain mysterious to this day. Perhaps he was indeed sick (though this is

Howard's first professional sale, "Spear and Fang," was published in the July 1925 issue of Weird Tales.

rather dubious), perhaps he felt the need of an "excuse" to justify his leaving the town, perhaps there were problems in the Howard household, but of course those other reasons would never have made their way into the local paper. It seems that the relations between Hester and Isaac had never been that great, and that she was reproaching her husband for his meager income. She who had spent most of her life in opulence and refinement was now living as a recluse in an isolated small town in Texas. If everybody in Cross Plains would later remember Doc Howard, always visiting his patients, wolfing down whatever they had on the table, then Hester Jane Howard was a cipher or an unknown quantity, and the number of guests at the Howard home seems to have dwindled over the years.

Two months later, on July 5, the *Cross Plains Review* trumpeted that "Dr. Howard is moving back to Cross Plains... The doctor's many patrons and friends are glad that he decided to return to Cross Plains." A few days later, it was Robert Howard's turn to leave home to settle in Brownwood. Here again, we simply do not know whether the return of the father caused the departure of the son, or the reverse, if Hester Jane was alone for a short while or not, and even if any of these events are related. The most probable hypothesis, though not backed by any evidence, is that Howard was now considering himself a full-time professional and wanted to fly on his own wings. Brownwood was the logical choice, as it wasn't far away, had all the facilities a writer needed, including large libraries, and this was where Vinson and Clyde Smith lived. Furthermore, it would be easier for Howard to be who he was in Brownwood. Many in Cross Plains saw him as the "town freak" and had a hard time understanding that writing for a living was a "real" job. As to the lurid covers of *Weird Tales*, they were not to everyone's tastes. It took not years, but decades, for Cross Plains to embrace Howard as one of its own.

Howard's career was still on an upward swing and his confidence grew by leaps and bounds: "On my return here I found a returned mss. from *Adventure*, with a line or two from the assistant editor, telling me to submit some more of my work, and soon after returning I got a letter from *Argosy*, accepting that story that I told you about. They said it was still far too long but they'd cut it down and make the necessary changes themselves. The day after getting that letter I got a check from them for $100. Also a letter from *Weird Tales* with the advance sheets of a story appearing in the next issue. Farnsworth said he intended publishing a sonnet in the next issue after that and then

"The Shadow Kingdom" which is a $100 story, and after that a shorter story. I believe he's paving the way to publish the serial I sold him, but of course I may be wrong." Very far from the doubt-riddled, aspiring writer of the preceding years, indeed.

We don't know a lot about Howard's life in Brownwood; logically so, since his main correspondent, Tevis Clyde Smith, was a Brownwood resident himself. One may suppose that the 1929 stock market crash and its consequences were factors in Howard moving back to Cross Plains shortly after Christmas, though, again, we simply don't know.

Howard's career took a new turn in early 1930 when he learned of the upcoming publication of two new pulp magazines that were right down his alley, and which offered a very real possibility of doubling his income: *Strange Stories* and *Oriental Stories*, both magazines to be launched by the same company which published *Weird Tales*, sparing him the need to build his reputation.

Strange Stories would be devoted to tales of adventure and history, with only a touch of the weird. In a matter of weeks, Howard wrote three stories which were of tremendous importance in his career, all of which were written specifically for the new publication: "Kings of the Night," "The Dark Man" and "The Gods of Bal-Sagoth". All three were immediately accepted by Farnsworth Wright. These tales were crucial in the development of Howard's writing style, and were the first to display so prominently and successfully what he is now most associated with: fast-moving adventure, epic or historical tales sprinkled with a touch of the weird.

When Howard heard the news of the launching of *Oriental Stories*, he was so excited that he interrupted his vacation and went back to Cross Plains. As was customary with him, he wrote a first tale mixing "oriental" elements (the new) with adventure (the old). After it was accepted, he began writing his first historical epics, ambitious and meticulously researched tales, betraying Howard's fascination with that thin, ever fluctuating line separating barbarism and civilization. The Crusades were his favorite topic, providing as they did a rich background and providing him with an immense playground and figures to play with. Unlike most of his contemporaries, Howard had no inclination to turn his tales into simplistic fables of good versus evil. Quite the contrary, his tales never portray a conquering Christianity. Division,. strife, and corruption are the common lot of his characters,

Howard's tale "Red Blades of Black Cathay" co-written with Tevis Clyde Smith made the cover of the February-March issue of Oriental Stories

barely holding on to their last fortresses, waiting for the inevitable final onslaught of their "Oriental" enemies. Civilization in these tales is always on the brink of annihilation, a fluttering candle at the mercy of the next gust of barbaric wind; stories peopled with broken men, leading hopeless lives of violence.

Nearly all of Howard's "Oriental" stories are masterpieces, in which his love of the material is plain: "There is no literary work, to me, half as zestful as rewriting history in the guise of fiction. I wish I was able to devote the rest of my life to that kind of work. I could write a hundred years and still there would be stories clamoring to be written, by the scores." Readers, however, were—and are—not so forgiving, seemingly not understanding that historical fiction is fiction before it is history, if it is that.

Strange Stories would never materialize (due to a dispute with a competitor) and the stories Howard had sold to the magazine were eventually published in *Weird Tales*, but the pebble had sent ripples to further shores: in early 1932, as he was on vacation in the south of Texas, Howard had the idea of Conan the Cimmerian, the character who would earn him fame and posterity. When he came back to Cross Plains, he had, willingly or not, stumbled upon the perfect solution to his aspirations: the Hyborian Age, a happy jumble of various geographical and historical periods in which no reader could take him to task for disregarding the details of history. Combining the bitter pessimism of his heroes, the clash of civilizations, and the eternal struggle between barbarism and civilization, the Conan tales became the privileged vessel for Howard to express his worldviews.

After a few alerts in 1931, when *Weird Tales* had briefly become a bi-monthly, Howard's professional situation took a turn for the worse in the spring of 1932. When the Fiction House line collapsed, *Fight Stories* and *Action Stories*, to which had been selling stories since 1929, went out of circulation, depriving him of a regular income. On the heels of that terrible blow came the news that *Strange Tales of Mystery and Terror*, a very promising and fast-paying market for weird stories, was also ceasing publication. Howard's financial situation became alarming in a matter of weeks, so much that he found himself unable to travel to New Orleans where H.P. Lovecraft was staying for a few days. The two men, who had begun corresponding in 1930, would never meet face to face.

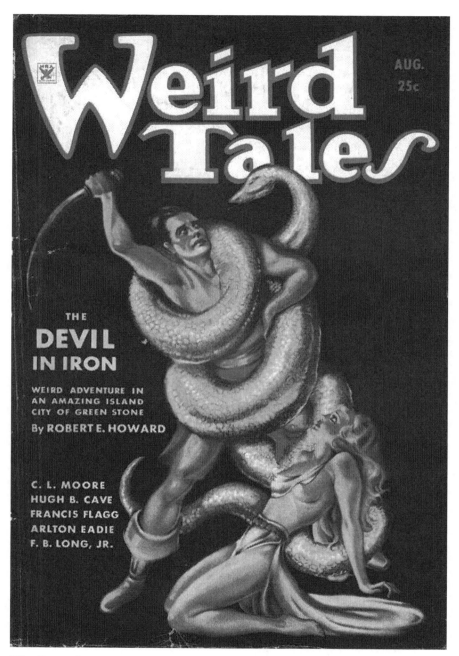

The Conan the Cimmerian story "The Devil in Iron" appeared on the cover of the August 1934 issue of Weird Tales. *Art by Margaret Brundage.*

With no real market other than *Weird Tales*—just like at the dawn of his career—Howard spent the next few weeks writing and selling as many Conan tales as possible. He was greatly helped in the process by the financial difficulties that were plaguing the magazine itself, which probably explain the hiring of a new cover artist, Margaret Brundage, who excelled at depicting the (naked) female body. She would soon become a star of the magazine, just like Howard, Clark Ashton Smith and that favorite of readers: Seabury Quinn. The Conan tales Howard penned during that period are not the best of the series: they were written to sell, often featuring gratuitous scenes whose only justification was to grab the cover design (cover stories received a bonus). In early 1933, the magazine had enough Conan tales in inventory to last until mid-1934. Howard could now concentrate on expanding his markets and he thus hired an agent to handle his stories on a non-exclusive basis: Otis Adelbert Kline, himself a former prolific pulp writer (notably for *Weird Tales*). Kline encouraged Howard to try new types of stories and thus new magazines. Howard complied by sending him a number of boxing stories, new or revamped from the unsold files, and embarked upon writing short westerns and detective stories. The western shorts were undistinguished standard pulp fare for the most part. As to the detective stories, Howard made no mystery that he didn't like *reading* them, much less *writing* them. The contrary would have been amazing, and one has a hard time picturing Howard writing convincing modern urban tales, as he had no experience at all in that area. His whodunit detective stories are uniformly bad, often relying on a single—and unconvincing—gimmick (a color-blind character, a hidden phonograph, etc.) with his detective reaching the key to the mystery with his fists. The few that have any merits are those that belong to that epitome of pulp genre: "weird menace" tales, that is to say fast-paced violent stories tinged with an atmosphere of the weird and the sadistic.

Howard's first truly successful forays with Kline were in the adventure department, many of his tales set in the rugged hills of Afghanistan, and for which Howard had resurrected a childhood character: Frank Gordon, nicknamed "El Borak" (the Swift), a nickname incidentally borrowed from a Rafael Sabatini tale Howard had read in his teens. Gordon was probably the modern hero Howard could readily identify with: rather small, dark-skinned, fighting on the side of the Afghans against the colonial and would-be empires (Russia and

England mostly). In other words, a Howard gone native, or a modern-day Bran Mak Morn. As the adventure pulps favored rather longish tales, Howard was at last able to make good money from those stories, plus he quickly learned to recycle his research into the Conan tales as well: the Hyborian country of Afghulistan, whose name is transparent enough, appeared in early 1934 as Howard was writing his first El Borak tales, for instance.

In the spring of 1933, Howard was introduced to Novalyne Price by his friend Tevis Clyde Smith, who had been a classmate of hers. Price had literary ambitions, and she was thus particularly anxious to meet the only man in the region who made his living exclusively from writing. She was rather startled to discover an individual who was about the opposite of what she had been expecting: "This man was a writer! Him? It was unbelievable. He was not dressed as I thought a writer should dress. His cap was pulled down low on his forehead. He had on a dingy white shirt and some loose-fitting brown pants that only came to his ankles and the top of his high-buttoned shoes." Price did enjoy the conversation, found Howard a particularly intriguing person, probably more than she would care to admit, but did not try to seek him out a second time.

At the same time, Howard at last found himself in the position to buy his own car. At a time when most of his fellow Cross Plains citizens were plunged in the dire conditions of the Great Depression, Howard was—again—making good money. After nearly a year of poor sales, his prospects were brighter. The story goes that Howard went to Fort Worth with his friend Lindsey Tyson and paid $350 in cash for the car. The seller almost fainted when he saw so much money.

Howard's financial success must have been of tremendous importance to the family. Many of Doc Howard's patients were unable to pay him other than in meat or vegetables. The success of Conan in the pages of *Weird Tales* is also a good indicator of the times—and what the character often represented—and still represents: he is the one that can survive the hardships and can manage by himself. He is the character the male reader would like to be, and the one the many female readers of *Weird Tales* would like to have for a companion.became those that lived on the fringes of, or outside, the law, such as Bonnie and Clyde, who had the sympathies of many at first, or even notorious gangsters who provided people with the alcohol

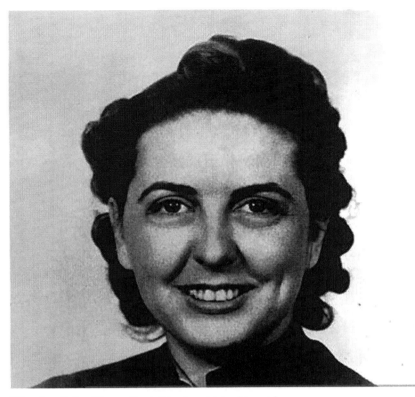

Novalyne Price, Howard's girlfriend and later biographer.

the government didn't want them to drink. Howard knew all that, understood it, and was in fact confronted by the same problems as his fellow Americans. In 1931, the two banks of Cross Plains went under only a few months apart, siphoning many of the local people's savings. Howard learned the lesson and would from then on deposit his savings in a postal account (hence backed by the government), thus ensuring that he would never suffer from such a fate again.

By June 1933, Howard's future thus seemed particularly bright: a car enabling him—at last!—to travel at will, good sales, excellent domestic prospects thanks to his hiring an agent, and a prospective new market abroad. He learned that his story "The Black Stone" had been published in England, included in a volume of the "Not at Night" series of books edited by Christine Campbell Thomson. Having become a member of the American Fiction Guild in 1932, Howard was now careful about his literary rights and paying close attention to new markets. An English publisher indicated that he would definitely consider a volume of stories for the British market. Howard selected nine of his best tales and sent them to England. It took the publisher several months to reply and explain that there was a "prejudice" against publishing a volume of short stories, but that he would consider a full-length novel on the same order. The hopes were slim, to say the least, but Howard gave it his best shot, and understandably so: book-form publication would be prestigious, and what was written for the British market could always be sold later in the USA, or vice-versa.

It took Howard some time to decide on the novel he wanted to write, before opting for a Conan tale. He devoted two months—from mid-March to mid-May 1934—to the writing of *The Hour of the Dragon*. From what we can gather, he didn't work on anything else during that time, not even sending a single letter to his friends and colleagues. He only took a few days off to welcome fellow pulpster E. Hoffmann Price, with whom he had been corresponding since 1929 (and best remembered today as the only writer to have met Howard, Lovecraft and Clark Ashton Smith).

1934 truly was the Howard year in *Weird Tales*: Of the twelve issues that came out that year, ten had a story (or chapters of a serial) by Howard, eight of those starring Conan, and his stories were cover-featured on four issues.

In August, Novalyne Price accepted a teaching position in Cross Plains and moved to town. One of the first things she did upon arriving was to give a phone call to renew her acquaintance with Howard. However, she did account for the Cerberus that was Hester Jane, who would inevitably answer every phone call and explain that her son was away or busy. Novalyne was not the kind of woman who would take no for an answer. Undeterred, she eventually went to the Howard home and rang. Bob Howard heard her and got out of the house, immediately inviting Novalyne for a ride. He quite clumsily tried to justify his mother's actions, obviously failing to convince Novalyne.

It would take only a few such dates before they fell in love, but the relation would soon become anything but a smooth ride. Just like all young people, they would go to the movies and have a soda afterward, but what they enjoyed most was arguing for the sake of it. Howard, the true storyteller, made history come alive under her eyes. She was impressed by the way he literally charmed her grandmother, and old people in general, whom he would question about life in the old days. She was delighted when he dressed up to please her, gave her cute and adorable nicknames, or would say one evening that he had designed a particularly beautiful moon just for her. She was appalled when he offered her the complete erotic works of French writer Pierre Louÿs for a Christmas gift. Howard's dedication—"The French have one gift—the ability to guild decay and change the maggots of corruption to the hummingbirds of poetry"—was a poor attempt at justification, and Novalyne would have had to be blind not to see what was on Howard's mind.

Howard was obviously torn between his domestic ideals, which were very much in accordance with the social codes of his era, and his attraction for Novalyne, who wasn't one to let conventions dictate her choices. She tried to convince him that the inhabitants of Cross Plains were not inherently hostile to him, and that if he would mingle a bit more with them, they would warm to him. Howard had been voluntarily avoiding social functions since he started building his career, and he felt that the inhabitants were genuinely antipathetic to him. That much can be inferred from E. Hoffman Price's visit to Cross Plains in 1934, when Howard stated that "nobody thinks I amount to much, so I am glad to have a chance to show these sons of ——s that a successful writer will drive a thousand miles to hell and gone out of his way to see me." Novalyne didn't realize that Howard was *tolerated* because he was the son of one of the most appreciated men in town: Dr. Howard.

The relationship between Howard and Novalyne Price would turn out to be too complicated for them, each entertaining at times thoughts of getting married, but not at the same moment. They stopped dating in mid-1935 (after Howard found out that she was also dating a friend of his, though not mentioning it to her), but would keep on seeing each other until February 1936, leading to some very difficult episodes, notably when Novalyne couldn't or wouldn't see Howard's pain as his mother was literally dying under his eyes. Hester Jane Howard's health wasn't good. It seems she had lied to her husband about her real age, pretending to be six years younger than she really was. The Ervin side of the family had long been believed to have been afflicted with tuberculosis, but recent research has shown that this was yet another fabrication by L. Sprague de Camp. Hester Jane *may* have suffered from tuberculosis or from cancer, or a combination of both, but we now know it was not

The famous photo of Howard with the fedora was taken during the period he was dating Novalyne Price.

hereditary. At any rate, her health became so preoccupying that she had to be rushed to the hospital on two instances in 1935, barely escaping with her life in both cases. Isaac Howard was a physician and knew perfectly well that his wife was dying, holding no illusion as to the final outcome. It seems, judging from Howard's letters, that he—not his father—was in charge of many of the special needs his mother now required on a daily basis, though Isaac was the physician in the family. Things became worse as time went by, and the two men had to hire a young woman—Kate Merryman—to alleviate the workload. Howard, who looked after his mother—drove her to the hospital, remained with her, drove her back—was constantly interrupted in his work. He quickly found himself unable to write for long stretches of time (several weeks in a row in early 1936, for instance). Meanwhile, *Weird Tales* was increasingly late in its payments and the hospital bills were accumulating. In May 1935, Howard had to write to the editor of the magazine, who owed him over $800, asking for a check. One year later, at the time of his death, Howard was owed $1,300 (over $25,000 in 2018 money). Howard had to turn to writing "spicy" (i.e. erotic) fiction under a pseudonym. This was fast work and the rates were excellent, but light-hearted as they were supposed to be, one can feel in the stories the tension and the frustrations that were gnawing at Howard. In the spring of 1936, he at long last managed to have a string of tales accepted by the prestigious *Argosy*, a lifelong ambition.

But the sands of time had run too low. Novalyne Price left Cross Plains for Louisiana in early 1936. Hester Howard's health took a turn for the worse. Howard found it impossible to concentrate on his work, to write, to make money.

Early in the morning of June 11, 1936, Hester Jane Howard sank into an irreversible coma. Howard asked the nurse on duty if there was the slightest chance she could become conscious again, to which the nurse replied in the negative. He had spent most of the night putting his papers in order, before rummaging through it and leaving the room in a mess. He went out of the house as he was used to doing every morning to go to the post office. His father had taken away all the guns stored in the house, but was unaware that his son had borrowed one from his friend Lindsey Tyson. Robert Howard opened the door of the car, stepped in, and fired a bullet through his brain.

Two physicians tried to revive him for the next hours, to no avail, and he died at 4 p.m. His mother gave her last on the next day, without having ever regained consciousness. A double funeral was organized for mother and son on June 14, who were buried in Brownwood.

The controversies surrounding Howard, his life and his work began appearing when he was not even buried. Isaac Howard, if recent biographical research is to be believed, is the first offender: he very probably destroyed the will in which his son left everything to his best friend, not to him. This means one of two things, one: either Howard thought his father would not survive his mother's death, just like him, or two: he had serious problems with him. The legend also goes that Isaac Howard salvaged Bob Howard's collection of pulp magazines, mis-

The last known photo of Robert E. Howard ca. Spring 1936.

handled by the people it had been given to, but this is inexact: he only saved those containing stories he thought could be published in book form and thus get money from their sale. We also know that he either made up (at worst) or embellished (at best) the story of his son's so-called suicide note. Last, he sent two or three stories (his letter is not very clear about it) to *Weird Tales*, explaining that he had just found an envelope and a piece of paper stating that those stories had just been completed and should be submitted to *Weird Tales*. Two of the stories in question dated from 1930 and the hypothetical third one from 1934, but there was no way Howard had retyped or rewritten them shortly before his death. Nonetheless, both tales were accepted by the magazine. Isaac Howard was obviously immensely affected by the tragedy which had struck his family, but he was at the same time particularly mercenary and did everything he could to derive as much profit as possible from his dead son's writings. A few days after the suicide, he had Robert's car cleaned. He then drove for several months the car in which his son had blown his brains out.

He eventually left Cross Plains in 1942 and settled in Ranger, in a clinic owned by close friends. The last years of his life were marked by an intense renewed interest in religion. A broken man, he died in 1944.

"It seems to me that many writers, by virtue of environments of culture, art and education, slip into writing because of their environments. I became a writer in spite of my environments."

– Robert E. Howard

Chapter Three
The Twenty Stories You Must Read (And Why)

Warning: 80-year-old spoilers ahead.

Note: The "recommended modern edition" volumes mentioned below were selected by choosing pure-text versions in all cases, and easily obtainable paperbacks whenever possible.

1. "The Shadow Kingdom"

Written: begun in the summer of 1926, completed in the summer of 1927.

First publication: *Weird Tales*, August 1929.

Recommended modern edition: *Kull: Exile of Atlantis*, Del Rey Books, 2006.

Synopsis: Kull, an orphan rescued and raised by an Atlantean tribe, leaves his adopted people to satisfy his thirst for power and glory. He eventually reaches the pinnacle of his dreams and mounts the throne of Valusia, an age-old decrepit empire living in the shadow of its former grandeur. Thinking his position secure, in spite of the opposition of the people who can't seem to accept his foreign origins, Kull is contacted by an emissary of the Pictish nation, who explains to him in plain terms that his throne is rocking under his feet and his life threatened: Serpent-Men are about to eliminate him and operate a coup d'état on Valusia. The Serpent-Men are formidable foes, shape-shifters who can take a human form at will. Kull, already isolated, can no longer trust anyone, and especially the few trusted men he was relying on, since they might have already been replaced by Serpent-Men. His only allies thus seem to be those Pictish barbarians who warned him of the imminent threat.

Illustation by Hugh Rankin of "The Shadow Kingdom" in Weird Tales *August 1929.*

Commentary: "The Shadow Kingdom" is the first story featuring Kull of Atlantis (unless one counts the fragment published as "Exile of Atlantis," which Howard discarded to write "The Shadow Kingdom"). The tale is a true study in paranoia. The protagonist—Kull—is an ambitious usurper, an orphan who broke every chain of "friendship, tribe and tradition" to achieve his ultimate dream: to become king of the fabled kingdom of Valusia. A foreigner and a parvenu, a barbarian with simple and straightforward ways, Kull is unable to understand the labyrinthine complexities of an empire crumbling upon itself. Forced to be wary of his own advisers, he finds himself obliged to put his trust in a savage Pict warrior who is exactly the man he would have probably become had he remained the barbarian he was fated to be.

This surprisingly mature tale, written by a Howard at only 21 years of age, lays the foundations of modern fantasy: pseudo-historical setting, weird and/or horrific elements, invented continents, and swashbuckling action. Contrary to popular belief, the tales of Kull (and later of Conan) do not take place in an imaginary universe, but in a distant, forgotten, era of our own past. At the time he was writing the story, Howard was convinced that Atlantis was an historical empire of Earth's distant past, and its sinking equally real.

This closeness between history, pseudo-history, and pure invention is one of the staples of Howardian fiction. By making his hero a barbarian of modest origins, Howard was harking back to the earliest heroes of mankind, whose births are almost always marked by tragedy and whose destiny promises to be extraordinary. A pivotal tale in Howard's career, since it was thanks to the sale of the story that he understood he would become a professional writer, but also for the fantasy and imaginative fiction genre as a whole.

2. "Solomon Kane" ("Red Shadows")

Written: January 1928
First publication: *Weird Tales*, August 1928, under the title "Red Shadows." Howard had initially titled his tale "Solomon Kane", but this was not satisfactory for the editor. It is unclear who gave the tale its more famous title.
Recommended modern edition: *The Savage Tales of Solomon Kane*, Del Rey Books, 2004.

Synopsis: Appearing out of the darkness, Solomon Kane discovers a very young woman, wounded and probably raped by the man she calls "Le Loup." As she breathes her last, Kane swears he will avenge her and that men shall pay for this deed. Thus begins a relentless manhunt that will take him months and across another continent, even though the woman was a complete stranger to him.

Commentary: "Solomon Kane" is the very first tale featuring the dour Puritan and a milestone for several reasons. First because of its form, which was problematic for the times. The editor of *Argosy* (the magazine to which the tale had first been submitted), explained the problem: "In some ways this story is very good, and in others it is rotten.... It starts out as a period story, & finally changes into a combination modern & medieval African jungle story. You can't mix periods & atmospheres like that. Stick to one or the other. Your story is disconnected, partly because of that same wandering from one period to another. There is too much that is unfinished or unexplained and too much that is miraculous. Then, there is absolutely no connection between the first & second parts. In one jump, you change from the

Weird Tales *January 1928 featuring the debut of Solomon Kane in "Red Shadows."* Cover by C. C. Senf

The August 1928 issue of Weird Tales *cover-featured the first Solomon Kane story. It is one of the most sought after issues in the collector market, and not only because of the Howard tale. Another writer made his professional debut in that same issue: the sixteen-year old Thomas Lanier Williams and his "The Vengeance of Nitocris." He would achieve fame a few years later under his pseudonym: Tennessee Williams.*

Middle Ages to Eugene O'Neill jungle stuff with no explanation save a vague intimation that there has been some kind of pursuit. If there has been such a chase or hunt, you can't omit it from your story.... What the readers want, and, incidentally, is hard to write is miracle stuff which can be explained to them by one means or another."

"Solomon Kane" is a groundbreaking tale *because* it follows none of those rules, *because* of the "defects" pointed out by the *Argosy* editor. Howard had understood or at least felt that the strength of his character resides precisely in this total scorn of the established conventions. We don't know who Kane is, where he comes from, or what his exact motivations are. He declares himself a Puritan and an instrument of God, but he may equally be afflicted with a form of madness. Howard himself described him as "a paranoid" in a letter. The Solomon Kane tales are not about Good vs. Evil either, a theme that is almost nowhere to be found in Howard. That Kane may think he is the armed hand of God is one thing, that there is any truth to his conviction is another. Howard never confirms nor denies. He appears when a crime has been committed, and will disappear as soon as the wrong has been righted, bringing with him his own brand of fanaticism, madness and justice. He anticipates Sergio Leone's Man with No Name (nearly 40 years early), but Howard is careful not to let the reader identify with his character, an austere man with an almost cadaveric countenance. This extraordinarily modern tale is a tour de force not because of its plot, but in its relentlessness, its unwillingness to submit to verisimilitude, pushing back the boundaries of the adventure and swashbuckling genres by adding a touch of the weird. Taking place in a half-serious, half-fantasy Elizabethan period, in wildly different geographical areas, the tale has been cited as a strong contender for Howard's first true fantasy tale rather than "The Shadow Kingdom."

3. "The Bulldog Breed"

Written: between September and October 1929.
First publication: *Fight Stories*, February 1930.
Recommended modern edition: *Grim Lands: The Best of Robert E. Howard Volume 2*, Del Rey Books, 2007.

Synopsis: After a violent dispute, the captain of the *Sea Girl*, a.k.a. "The Old Man", has had enough and announces that he can no longer tolerate the presence of Steve Costigan's dog onboard. Costigan refuses to abandon his dog and thus leaves the ship with the animal, ready to begin a new life. But of course, Costigan is unable to stay away from trouble for any extended period of time.

Commentary: "The Bulldog Breed" doesn't belong to any of Howard's famed fantasy cycles. It is a boxing story, and a funny one at that. When Howard wrote the tale, boxing was incredibly popular. *Fight Stories*, which had begun in 1928, was devoted exclusively to "prize-fighting yarns" (as Howard put it). He had dozens of stories published in the magazine (and its sister publications), many of which have stood the test of time remarkably well. "The Bulldog Breed" is usually considered to be the best tale in the series, perfectly summing up, as it does, many aspects of Howard's philosophy of life. More often than not (systematically?), Howard's heroes are said to be violent men who will ultimately triumph because they are the strongest ones around, and can thus impose their will on others (and sometimes hear the lamentations of their women). Nothing could be more off the mark. Physical force in Howard—and this is true for *all* his creations—is only what enables the character to remain alive, to survive at the end and to escape death. These characters have, in their immense majority, no intention whatsoever to exert any form of domination on others, to reign as tyrants, or to conquer. Steve Costigan is a perfect illustration: he is the champion of his ship—not because he is the best fighter aboard, or the strongest, but because he is the one that won't go down, refusing to accept defeat. He is one of those "men of iron" who fascinated Howard; not so much remarkable athletes than freaks of nature, fighters almost frightening in their ability to take punishment and still stand on their feet.

In a body of work that is mostly dark and pessimistic, Howard's humoristic tales show several distinctive traits. The first is Howard's style and his use of slang and stereotypes. The second, and probably most important, is the use of the absolutely unreliable narrator that is Steve Costigan, ready to all exaggerations and deformations, the ideal sucker for any cheap ploy and perfect fall guy for any would-be *femme fatale* bent on manipulating him. If you like Damon Runyon and his Guys and Dolls tales, chances are you'll like Costigan.

The (rather surprising) common theme between the Costigan tales stories is that of family, more or less openly stated. Behind Steve Costigan, his bulldog Mike, the Old Man and the *Sea Girl* can be seen the projection of a happy (if often dysfunctional) family, where Mike is the (re)incarnation of Patches, Howard's beloved dog (who had died a few months before he launched the series), the Old Man being the father of the house, and the ship turned into a maternal symbol: "Since I growed up, the *Sea Girl's* been the only home I knowed, and though I've left her from time to time to prowl around loose or to make a fight tour, I've always come back to her."

"The Bulldog Breed" is pure Howard—one of those tales without which it is impossible to really apprehend his personality: Costigan's loyalty to his dog is typical Howard—"a man that won't stand by his dog is lower down than one which won't stand by his fellow man"—giving the story a depth which elevates it above most other tales of the series. With those elements in mind, the following lines by Costigan have powerful resonance: "I tell you, the average man has got to be fighting for somebody else besides hisself. It's fighting for a flag, a nation, a woman, a kid or a dog that makes a man win." A declaration that would find its echo years later when Howard told Novalyne Price: "You have a great cause. For life to be worth living, a man—a man or woman—must have a great love or a great cause. I have neither."

4. "Hawks of Outremer"

Written: September 1930.
First publication: *Oriental Stories*, Spring 1931.
Recommended modern edition: *Sword Woman and other Historical Adventures*, Del Rey Books, 2011.

Synopsis: While many think him dead in those troubled times of the Third Crusade, Cormac FitzGeoffrey makes so unexpected a comeback that he is almost mistaken for a ghost. Soon after, he learns of the passing of one his—all too few—close friends, and that those responsible for his death are another Crusader, baron von Gonler, and Saladin. Cormac leaves on the spot to avenge his friend.

Commentary: Kull, literary ancestor to Conan? No, it is in this tale, the one with which Howard truly began an impressive collaboration with *Oriental Stories* (after a lukewarm adventure tale) that he laid the foundations of what would ultimately become Conan and the Hyborian Age, much more than with the tales of Kull of Atlantis. The Crusades, as depicted by most of his contemporaries, portrayed valorous knights flying to the rescue of an imperiled Christendom, whose Outremer possessions were threatened by an enemy as despicable as ruthlessly evil. There is no such thing in Howard.

Howard's tales were dark and pessimistic, close in tone to the works of Harold Lamb, one of the star contributors to the prestigious *Adventure*, and whom Howard admired immensely. But while the stories published in the venerable magazine were well crafted, they also showed definite restraint. With Howard, it was anything goes, especially violent bloodshed and raw emotions: "One of the main things I like about Farnsworth Wright's magazines, is you don't have to make your heroes such utter saints," confided Howard. As to Cormac himself, he is everything but a noble knight, brought up in the ideals of chivalry: "At twelve, I was running wild with shock-head kerns on the naked fens—I wore wolfskins, weighed near to fourteen stone, and had killed three men."

As was the case for Kane, the extreme violence of the FitzGeoffrey tales (added to the unlikeable temperament of the character himself), made them impossible to sell other than in the magazines edited by Farnsworth Wright. Whoever has read this story but once can't forget the confrontation scene between von Gonler and Cormac. Evolving in a world shaken by the convulsions of crumbling and decaying empires, where "barbarians" and "civilized" are all too often indistinguishable, Cormac, a character of Celtic stock, with "volcanic" blue eyes, and who swears at times by "Crom," is without the shadow of a doubt the true literary ancestor to the Cimmerian. He is what the Conan series would have been, had Howard been in a position—as he devoutly wished—to earn enough money writing historicals: unrelenting, often epic, violent, and uncompromising.

5. "The Black Stone"

Written: November 1930.
First publication: *Weird Tales*, November 1931.
Recommended modern edition: *Crimson Shadows: The Best of Robert E. Howard Volume 1*, Del Rey Books, 2007.

Synopsis: The narrator is intrigued by the mention of a mysterious monolith in Von Junzt's *Nameless Cults*. He decides to travel to Hungary and see for himself, as he is convinced he has established a link between the monolith, a darksome cult, and verse written by Justin Geoffrey, the "mad poet."

"Death to you, Nazarene!" he yelled.

Hawks of Outremer
By ROBERT E. HOWARD
Cormac, the Irish-Norman Crusader, meets Saladin, Lion of Islam, under stirring circumstances—a red-blooded story

"Hawks of Outremer" interior illustration.

Commentary: What can one say about "The Black Stone"? Reprinted dozens of times since its initial publication in the pages of *Weird Tales*, this magisterial short story is the perfect fusion of the style and themes of two of the most important writers in the domain of imaginative fiction of the first half of the twentieth century: Howard and Lovecraft.

Howard had recently initiated a correspondence with the man from Providence, but was in awe of Lovecraft and his erudition. In his first letters, he was almost excusing himself for writing the kind of stories he was selling, instead of authoring Lovecraftian or "cosmic" horror. For a number of weeks, Howard was convinced that he had found his true calling in literature, the key to "approach real literature," and thus began aping Lovecraft, trying to emulate his style, but also his worst excesses. Some of the tales Howard penned in that pe-

riod rank among his worst efforts. However, "The Black Stone" is a marvelous achievement that helps us forget all the other half-baked efforts. It is a Howardian tale, displaying the Texan's fascination for history (the allusion to the Turkish invasions) set in a very Lovecraftian world, and told by an equally Lovecraftian protagonist. It is this last point which elevates the story above a simple exercise in style. By featuring a protagonist who was a scholar instead of Howard's usual footloose wanderer, Howard was writing about a character that was much closer to who he *really* was than any Conan or Solomon Kane, even if he would go to great lengths to show that he was not, first and foremost, an intellectual. Cross Plains, the small Texas town where he lived, was far from a welcoming place for a writer in the 1920s and 30s. Howard had to fit in, one way or another, and he would at times adopt the attitude and expressions of a worker, a wordsmith (emphasis on "smith"), a proletarian writer—hence somewhat akin to his fellow citizens. This was probably a necessary protection in an environment where most people would never consider writing for a living a "real" job, in an era when Howard simply didn't know of anyone else in the region making a living from his or her typewriter.

Between the intellectual narrator and the tormented personality of Justin Geoffrey, it isn't difficult to recognize Howard himself in some passages. The portrait of Geoffrey we can read in another—unfinished—tale written at the same time leaves little doubt as to who Howard was really writing about: "In another family, he had certainly been encouraged and had blossomed forth as an infant prodigy. But his unspeakably prosaic family saw in his scribbling only a waste of time and an abnormality which they thought they must nip in the bud.... But the abnormalities which his family thought they saw in his poetry were not those which I see. To them, anyone who does not make his living by selling potatoes is abnormal."

By daring to project another facet of himself on paper, Howard delivers a tale in which his preoccupations meet—for once—those of Lovecraft, without disavowing himself. Even the most hardcore Lovecraft fanatics hold "The Black Stone" in high esteem, and the text is regularly hailed as the most Lovecraftian story written by a writer other than Lovecraft himself.

6. "The Horror from the Mound"

Written: late June, early July 1931.
First publication: *Weird Tales*, May 1932.
Recommended modern edition: *The Horror Stories of Robert E. Howard*, Del Rey Books, 2008.

Synopsis: Steve Brill, tenant farmer without a cent before him, ekes out a miserable living on the small patch of land he desperately tries to cultivate. We are in Texas, during the Great Depression. As the story opens, he is observing once again the strange routine of his neighbor, a taciturn Mexican, who methodically steers around a mound standing on the path that leads him to his home. When he decides to ask the reason for this, the Mexican reluctantly explains that the place is haunted. Brill, somewhat stubborn, somewhat racist, comes to the conclusion that his neighbor is not telling the whole truth and that the mound may in fact be an ancient burial place, in which—maybe—there's gold to be found.

Commentary: Howard had the utmost difficulties selling this story, which was sent back several times before being accepted by *Weird Tales*. "The Horror from the Mound" is now widely hailed as a minor classic, the tale that inaugurated the subgenre of the "weird western." On top of that, it is Howard's first successful western, devoid of any of the clichés that usually plague the genre. The tale owes its strength to the excellent atmosphere and color touch. Howard, for the first time in his career, writes about something he knows first-hand. This is where he lives, these people are those he can meet almost any day, who live but a few miles from him. But the real literary accomplishment is that Howard succeeds yet another time to mix two genres, which, logically, should not meet: the realistic western and the vampire tale, as seen and filtered through the lens of Howard's experience.

It was simply impossible for Howard to be a derivative writer. When he consciously tried to imitate other writers, as happened a few times, it didn't work ("The Black Stone" being the only counter-example, though it isn't really entirely derivative). A few weeks after having probably reread Bram Stoker's *Dracula*, and just after seeing Bela Lugosi onscreen (probably in March 1931), Howard thus penned his first vampire tale. But it was out of the question for him to write about the conventional Victorian era blood-sucker: Howard simply imported the theme, Americanized it, bringing the undead to an environment that had never been his, that *couldn't* be his, one would almost be tempted to say. Blending the vampire lore and the peculiar geographical and historical contexts, Howard wrought a tale that is simply brilliant. Unfortunately, not everyone thought so. Just like Solomon Kane (who couldn't be allowed to jump from one continent to another between a chapter and the next), some readers just couldn't accept the "liberties" taken by Howard. A disgruntled reader thus explained in *Weird Tales'* reader column that the story contained "no less than four flagrant breaches of accepted vampire tradition. Are we to believe, simply because Mr. Howard so informs us, that vampires can now remain alive for years, underground, without their customary nightly feast of human blood? Or that they can be confined to their graves by a mere slab of rock? Or that they now find it necessary to engage in rough-house wrestling bouts with their prospective victims? Improvements are always in order, but Mr. Howard's new type of vampire is certainly no improvement!"

Yet another example that helps us better understand why, and how, Howard came to create Conan's Hyborian Age as a means to free himself from such "constraints" and remarks. Sadly, there's still no formula for freeing oneself from self-righteous "fans".

7. "Lord of Samarcand"

Written: September or October 1931.
First publication: *Oriental Stories*, Spring 1932.
Recommended modern edition: *Sword Woman and other Historical Adventures*, Del Rey Books, 2011

Synopsis: As the titanic battle that saw the armies of Bayazid crushing the Franks, Ak Boga the Tatar is witness to a strange episode: a Scottish knight challenging and killing in a duel a nobleman whose recklessness and stupidity was instrumental in bringing about the rout of the knights. As the Scotsman sees Ak Boga and prepares to kill him, too, the Tatar calmly explains that he is no foe of his, quite the contrary, and that his own master, Timur, is also an enemy of Bayazid. He invites the Scotsman to follow him, with a promise to take revenge on Bayazid in the future.

Commentary: Little doubt when reading this bitter epic that Howard was born to write historicals. His protagonist is one of his many heroes broken by life, warring and pursuing oblivion in a world that offers no solace and no future. "There isn't a gleam of hope in it. It's the fiercest and most sombre thing I ever tried to write. A lot of milksops—maybe—will say it's too savage to be realistic, but to my mind, it's about the most realistic thing I ever attempted. But it's the sort of thing I like to write—no plot construction, no hero or heroine, no climax in the accepted sense of the word, all the characters complete scoundrels, and everybody double-crossing everybody else." And once again, the readers' reaction is worth noting. The powerful strength of the story was overlooked by some, who seemed bent on attacking Howard on the "veracity" of the historical facts: "Some of the readers took exception to my making Tamerlane a drinking man. I expected to be attacked on other scores—on Bayazid's suicide, which of course never took place—about my version of Timour's death—more particularly I expected to be denounced because of the weapon my character used in that slaying. There were firearms in the world then, and had been for some time, but they were of the matchlock order. I doubt if there were any flintlock weapons in Asia in 1405. But the readers pounced on to the point I least expected—the matter of Muhammadan drunkards. They maintained that according to the Koran, Moslems never drank." Such reactions also undoubtedly played a very important part in the following months, when Howard conceived the "Hyborian Age," that is to say a pseudo-historical era of our world, in which he could write as many historicals as he wanted, but pretending they were not, and thus preventing any such reactions from his readers.

8. **"Worms of the Earth"**

Written: circa late 1931.
First publication: *Weird Tales*, November 1932.
Recommended modern edition: *Bran Mak Morn: The Last King*, Del Rey Books, 2005.

Synopsis: When Rome pushes things too far by crucifying one of his subjects under his very eyes, Bran Mak Morn, king of the Pictish

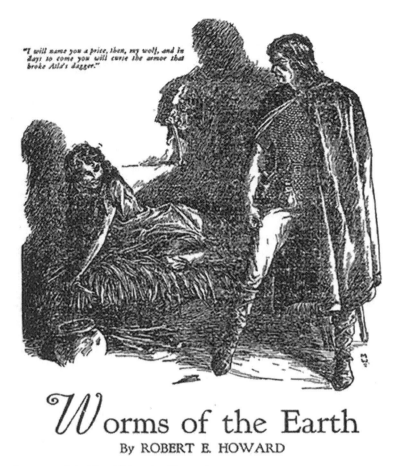

"*I will name you a price, then, my wolf, and in days to come you will curse the armor that broke Atla's dagger.*"

Worms of the Earth
By ROBERT E. HOWARD

"Worms of the Earth" interior illustration.

nation, swears to kill Titus Sulla, the military governor responsible for the execution. And to achieve that goal, Bran will go to the limits of horror and conclude a pact with Atla, the witch, and the underground beings called the Worms of the Earth, at the risk of losing his humanity and his sanity in the process.

Commentary: The perfect blend of Howardian historical fantasy and lovecraftian horror, composed a few weeks before Howard had the idea of Conan of Cimmeria. "Worms of the Earth" is one of these all-too-rare stories that will haunt you long after you have finished it. Howard doesn't spare the reader anything in that somber tale centered on the tragic figure of Bran, confronted with the horrors of

Roman occupation, to the slow and inevitable decay of his people, to the futility of his relentless efforts to save the Picts, already on the brink of oblivion, and last but certainly not least, to the lengths (or rather depths) he finds himself ready to go to, fully aware of the consequences on his future and that of the Pictish nation. Lovecraft, perceptive as he often was, couldn't praise the story enough.

If one had to decide which character was closest to Howard among his many creations, it wouldn't be Conan or Solomon Kane, but Bran Mak Morn, whose eventual defeat is a certainty, even to himself. Far from admiring the gigantic, blonde and blue-eyed barbarians he is so often readily associated with, Howard had a lifelong admiration and fascination for the Picts: "In reading of the Picts, I mentally took their side against the invading Celts and Teutons, whom I knew to be my type and indeed, my ancestors. My interest, especially in my early boyhood, in these strange Neolithic people was so keen, that I was not content with my Nordic appearance, and had I grown into the sort of man, which in childhood I wished to become, I would have been short, stocky, with thick, gnarled limbs, beady black eyes, a low retreating forehead, heavy jaw, and straight, coarse black hair—my conception of a typical Pict."

9. "The Phoenix on the Sword"

Written: February 1932.
First publication: *Weird Tales*, December 1932.
Recommended modern edition: *The Coming of Conan the Cimmerian*, Del Rey Books, 2003.

Synopsis: Conan the Cimmerian is king of Aquilonia, but his situation is far from being an enviable one. He knows the people grumble behind his back. More importantly, a quatuor of ambitious rebels are actively working toward his downfall, each for his own reasons. The plot takes a very different turn once the slave of one of the conspirators chances upon his long-lost ring of power, a slave by the name of Thoth-amon, who used to be a great sorcerer in Stygia.

Commentary: "The Phoenix on the Sword" is far from being a perfect text, but its presence in this list is justified by its status alone, since this is the tale that introduced Conan the Cimmerian to the world, created (or modernized) a whole genre, and was thus the story by which Howard earned his fame. "Phoenix" is the rewrite of an unsold 1929 Kull tale titled "By this Axe I rule!", which Howard unearthed from his archives in early 1932, after having spent some time in South Texas, where he had had the idea of Conan. Howard updated his unsold tale by getting rid of the sentimental subplot and adding a more pronounced fantasy element. Mixing an imaginary era of our past (the "Hyborian Age," a sampling of different historical and geographical eras of our planet under thinly disguised names), drawing maps of this new world, writing a history of how these kingdoms and empires came to be, Howard codified and crystallized in a matter of weeks most of the elements that have since become the staples of the fantasy genre.

Critics can discuss what existed before, what Howard owes—or not—to such Victorian or post-Victorian fantasy writers as William Morris or Lord Dunsany. They can argue as to the merits—or lack of them—of Howard's prose, they can discuss Gilgamesh and Tolkien, no one can deny that modern fantasy (even if you want to call it heroic fantasy or sword and sorcery, appellations as reductive as they are misleading), was born with "The Phoenix on the Sword."

Thoth-amon the Stygian sorcerer has become, in the pastiches, the comics and elsewhere, Conan's arch-enemy, which he is absolutely not. More, he cares nothing about the Cimmerian. We don't even know if he is aware of Conan's presence as his revenge is exacted, not upon the Aquilonian king, but on the conspirators. Conan would have been, at best, collateral damage. This won't change in any of the future stories since, contrary to popular belief, "Phoenix" marks the only appearance of Thoth-amon in the series. (He is mentioned in another tale, but, once again, not in relation to Conan.) In fact, the Conan stories are very rarely about the Cimmerian himself. More often than not, he is simply the catalyzer, the man whose barbaric presence will help put events in motion, or will help accelerate their outcome.

Character motivation, in Howard's fiction in general and in the Conan stories in particular, is purely human: sex, power, money, or revenge. Thoth-amon is simply bent on exacting revenge, to repair what he considers a wrong. He is not there to unleash the Reign of Evil on the Hyborian Age. Ascalante, head of the conspiracy is quite similar to Conan in many respects: a bold adventurer who is about to strike for the crown for egotist motives. As to Rinaldo, he is this tale's Justin Geoffrey, the minstrel whose Hamlet-like madness induces him to stab a king simply because he happens to be king.

Conan's Hyborian Age is a mostly realistic world, seeped and draped in (pseudo-)historical verisimilitude, a mostly anthropomorphous universe (peopled not with dragons and trolls, but with giant snakes, enormous hyenas and lecherous sorcerers). The Conan stories are an alternate (or more modern) version of the historical or swashbuckling tales, sprinkled with a few weird elements and less ice than in some modern counterparts.

10. "The Frost-Giant's Daughter"

Written: February 1932.
First publication: (as "Gods of the North," slightly rewritten as an "Amra of Akbitana" tale), in *The Fantasy Fan*, March 1934.
Recommended modern edition: *The Coming of Conan the Cimmerian*, Del Rey Books, 2003.

Synopsis: In the aftermath of a battle opposing Vanir and Æsir in the frozen wastes of the North, Conan the Cimmerian, who has fought alongside the men of Vanaheim, kills the last of his opponents. As he is still stunned from the battle, a young woman, entirely naked, appears in front of him...

Commentary: "The Frost Giant's Daughter" is the second tale Howard wrote featuring his new character, Conan the Cimmerian. The tale is a very short one, written in a poetic, almost dreamlike, style. It was rejected outright by Farnsworth Wright, the editor at *Weird Tales*, who said he "didn't care" for it. When one studies what Wright objected to in some other Howard stories, it becomes easy to deduce what he disliked about that particular tale: the overly explicit sexual elements. *Weird Tales*, if one is to believe the readers' column, had a rather high percentage of female readers, and many of those saw Conan as a sort of romantic anti-hero, a violent barbarian, but who was, at the end of the day, quite chivalric. A Hyborian Age Han Solo, rough, but likable. "The Frost Giant's Daughter" shows us that Conan wouldn't have thought twice about shooting first to kill Greedo. Mesmerized, bewitched, dazed after receiving one blow too

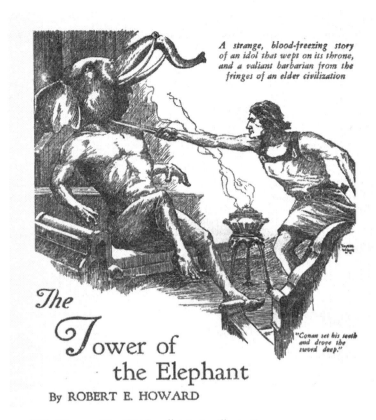

A strange, blood-freezing story of an idol that wept on its throne, and a valiant barbarian from the fringes of an elder civilization

The

Tower of the Elephant

By ROBERT E. HOWARD

"Conan set his teeth and drove the sword deep."

"The Tower of the Elephant" interior illustration.

many… maybe. Still, Conan spends most of the story running after what he believes to be a beautiful woman with one intention only: to crush her in the snow and rape her. Here is what was probably too much for editor Farnsworth Wright, even for such an outré magazine as *Weird Tales*. Conan is anything but a chivalrous antihero. Yes, he will behave on most occasions, but his feral nature is never very far below the surface. Scratch it at your own risk.

11. "The Tower of the Elephant"

Written: March 1932.
First publication: *Weird Tales*, March 1933.
Recommended modern edition: *The Coming of Conan the Cimmerian*, Del Rey Books, 2003.

Synopsis: A brawl erupts in a crowded tavern of the Maul, in the seedy section of an unnamed town. Among the customers from many countries and shady walks of life, a young barbarian has caused the ire of a Kothian thief when he bragged that a bold thief could steal the Heart of the Elephant, the mysterious and famed gem held by the sorcerer Yara, up in the recesses of the tower that is his stronghold. During the brawl, the tavern is plunged in darkness. When someone eventually lights a candle, the Kothian is dead and the Cimmerian fled... toward the tower of the Elephant.

Commentary: "The Tower of the Elephant" is the first truly satisfying Conan tale. It was the fourth in the series, but in-between the third and this one, Howard had written the pseudo-historical article "The Hyborian Age" and drawn two maps of the Hyborian countries. He had, in short, worked hard to detail the world his characters evolve in and lend it a greater aspect of verisimilitude. Many of those elements found their way in "Tower of the Elephant" (via Yagkosha's monologue and the long exposition of the various characters and Hyborian nationalities at the onset of the tale). Despite all this expository material, the story almost functions as a fairy tale, so palpable is the sense of wonder throughout. Howard waxes poetic, and the plot moves at a brisk pace, systematically surprising us by going in entirely unexpected directions, slowly leaving the down-to-earth preoccupations of the thieves and cut-throats to rise to the heights of the tower and cosmic considerations. One guesses that Howard went on with the tale without trying too hard to give it a rational ending. Moving and eminently poetic, "The Tower of the Elephant" is the first exceptional story featuring Conan.

12. "The Shadow of the Vulture"

Written: June/July 1932.
First publication: *Magic Carpet Magazine*, January 1934.
Recommended modern edition: *Sword Woman and other Historical Adventures*, Del Rey Books, 2011.

Synopsis: Vienna. 1529. The hosts of Soliman the Magnificent are nearing the gates of the city. Oblivious to these portentous events, Gottfried von Kalmbach wakes with some difficulty after a night of debauchery in a tavern. Minutes later, while he is still very much intoxicated, he is forced into action as the outriders of Soliman arrive on the scene, led by Mikhal Oglu, the Vulture, the Sultan's ruthless raider. And Soliman has put a price on Von Kalmbach's head.

Commentary: The siege of Vienna in 1529. The battle for the city that was the key to Europe for Soliman the Magnificent. A subject that was eminently tailored for Howard, and which resulted in a masterpiece, featuring two of his most memorable characters ever, and a series of splendid passages. Before embarking on the writing, Before starting to write, Howard researched the subject extensively but it was not in a history book he found his protagonist Gottfried von Kalmbach. The half-courageous, half-pitiful drunkard, black sheep of an illustrious family, who long ago traded any fame and glory ideals for the nearest flagon of wine was obviously inspired by Shakespeare's Falstaff. And in Sonya of Rogatino, Howard gave Gottfried the perfect companion. So-called (imaginary) sister to (the real) Roxelana, a concubine of Soliman, Sonya is a fiery redhead. A skilled and boisterous warrior, she is definitely attractive: "She stood as a man might stand, booted legs braced wide apart, thumbs hooked into her girdle, but she was all woman." She is the rock against which Gottfried von Kalmbach will first crash, then hold on to while he tries to recapture his dignity as the world around him is plunged in apocalypse. If the character of Gottfried was not destined to become famous, Sonya's fate was rather exceptional. When Roy Thomas—the writer of Marvel Comics' *Conan the Barbarian* comic book—decided to adapt the story and transform it into a Conan story in the process, he simply took the whoring and guzzling Gottfried as he was, erasing some of the more comical and pitiful aspects of the character to turn him into a Marvel Comics Conan. Red Sonya became Red Sonja (a slight "Hyborian" variation on her name). As illustrated by Barry Smith, the character was quite faithful to the original Howard tale, but Sonja wouldn't become a hit until her next appearances, when it was decided she would be clad in a chainmail bikini and leather boots. The idea met with tremendous approval from the libidinous and mostly male teenage public that constituted Marvel's core readership, and Red Sonja became an authentic kitsch icon. Sadly, people took Howard to task for having created such a goofy character, reinforcing the "macho writer" image that was already plaguing his reputation. So

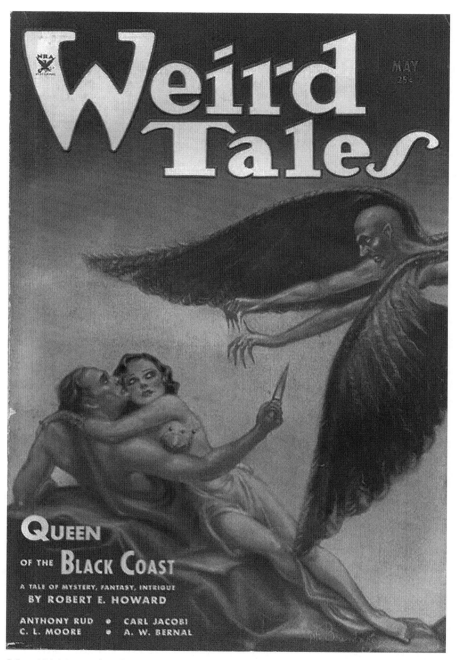

May 1934 issue of Weird Tales *with* "Queen of the Black Coast" *cover by Brundage.*

it's worth repeating that Sonya's first and only appearance was in Vienna, in 1529, in one of Howard's best historical tales.

13. "Queen of the Black Coast"

Written: July/August 1932.
First publication: *Weird Tales*, May 1934.
Recommended modern edition: *The Coming of Conan the Cimmerian*, Del Rey Books, 2003.

Synopsis: Conan arrives at breakneck speed on the wharf and jumps aboard the *Argus*, the ship of Master Tito, bound for the kingdom of Cush. The Cimmerian explains that he was fleeing the law, after having escaped from the tribunal where he was being judged for having helped a friend. A short while later, a sail appears on the horizon and Tito realizes soon enough that this is the *Tigress*, the ship of Bêlit, Queen of the Black Coast, the "wildest she-devil unhanged." Tito's men prepare for the oncoming boarding.

Commentary: "Queen of the Black Coast" is one of the more famous Conan tales, and rightly so, mostly due to Bêlit, which popular imagination (no doubt helped by Marvel Comics) has since transformed into Conan's major or unique "true love." The text is mesmerizing and its construction evokes an initiatory plunge into the depths of the unconscious, beginning in the nightmare that are civilized ways in Argos to find balance in the vicarious life of a pirate and concluding once again in a nightmarish fashion, this time by sailing back a sullen river up to the heart of darkness, where the pirates will meet their doom in the form of what was once the ultimate form of civilization, since fallen back to the abysses of utmost savagery, thus concluding the cycle of generations.

Bêlit is everything but the "true love" of Conan, and their relation is anything but romantic. She is first and foremost a greedy and power-hungry warrior, whose relationship with Conan is tinged with more than a hint of sadomasochism. The funerals Conan organizes for her in the last paragraphs are not those of a heartbroken lover, but those a Viking warrior would offer a fallen shield-brother or sword-sister. It is the fellow warrior Conan mourns the most, not the lost lover. (As to that tear Conan supposedly sheds, you are probably remembering the Marvel Comics version.)

The imagery of the text, with its triumphant white woman kinging it naked over a crew of black warriors, is powerful and archetypal. It also contributes to date the tale back to the late Victorian era and the first half of the twentieth century, evoking such classic characters as Rider Haggard's She, or La of Opar in E.R. Burroughs' Tarzan novels.

14. "The Man on the Ground"

Written: somewhere between October and December 1932.
First publication: *Weird Tales*, July 1933.
Recommended modern edition: *Grim Lands: The Best of Robert E. Howard Volume 2*, Del Rey Books, 2007.

Synopsis: An undying hate opposes Cal Reynolds and Esau Brill. Their feud has been going on for years, though neither remembers exactly what started it. A dispute over something, which somehow grew and took monstrous and ghastly proportions, to the point of obliterating every other aspect of their respective lives. As the story opens, both men have just stumbled upon each other in an isolated spot. A shot is fired.

Commentary: "The Man on the Ground" is a very short tale written with the most extreme care, and with a dryness particularly well adapted to its subject matter. This is Howard's Texas, the background he was deeply familiar with, with its cattlemen, its peculiar geography, vegetation, and its feuds. The theme and story are deceptively simple (as is often the case in Howard), but he operates a masterful twist on the conventions of the genre, turning the hero of the tale into… something he couldn't logically be. Cal Reynolds is a man who doesn't really live. He simply is, and his whole existence is summed up by his hate of Brill (and vice versa). This visceral hate of the other slowly becomes the only thing that animates him, in the strictest sense of the word. He is defined by it, and his earthly body has become but a shell, a human vehicle for the incarnation of his hate. He is hate personified, and he can only "die" when it has found release in the killing of Brill. We are in presence of a theme that runs throughout the entirety of Howard's body of fiction, in which some individuals seem defined and animated only by a hatred which literally consumes them. One is reminded of the short discussion between two warriors whose entire life has been dedicated to the wiping out of their foes, in the Conan tale "Red Nails." One asks the other what will happen to them after their enemies have been disposed of: "Will it not seem strange, to have no foes to fight? All my life I have fought and hated the Xotalancas. With the feud ended, what is left?" To which his companion has no answer: "Xatmec shrugged his shoulders. His thoughts had never gone beyond the destruction of their foes. They could not go beyond that."

15. "Sword Woman"

Written: very probably in June or July 1934.
First publication: *REH: Lone Star Fictioneer* #2, Nemedian Chronicles, Summer 1975.
Recommended modern edition: *Sword Woman and other Historical Adventures*, Del Rey Books, 2011.

Synopsis: Normandy, France, early sixteenth century. Today is the day the red-headed Agnes of the village of La Fere will marry the man her father, an ex-soldier with a shady past, has chosen for her. As the ceremony is about to begin, Agnes' sister comes to her. She implores Agnes not to follow her path, not to repeat her mistake. She, who used to be a beautiful woman, has become in a few short years and after a forced wedding, a crooked and haggard peasant woman, with none of her spirit left. She gives Agnes a knife, begging her sister to avoid the fate she had to suffer. But far from killing herself (as was obviously her sister's suggestion), she goes to her future husband and acts in the flash of an instant: "My dagger was sheathed in his pig's heart before he realized I had struck, and I yelped with mad glee to see the stupid expression of incredulous surprize and pain flood his red countenance, as I tore the dagger free and he fell, gurgling like a stuck pig, and spouting blood between his clawing fingers—to which clung petals from his bridal chain." Seconds later, Agnes is running away and fleeing home forever.

Commentary: Even today, "Sword Woman" remains a powerful text (though far from perfect). That Howard, whom many still think of as a misogynist, wrote this text in 1934 is simply unbelievable, given his environment. Catherine L. Moore, a fabled *Weird Tales* writer he would send the story to a few months later (probably after it had been rejected by several magazines) couldn't praise it enough. At the time, Moore was writing a series for *Weird Tales* featuring her own red-haired heroine, Jirel of Joiry. By an amazing coincidence, the two writers had independently created strikingly similar characters at the same time. Howard, who was increasingly dissociating himself from the magazine and from the genre, wrote his tale with a straight adventure market in mind, but it failed to sell. This was probably because "Sword Woman" was a little too different and daring for the time, not because of the tale's liberties with verisimilitude (Agnes becoming a seasoned swordswoman in a matter of pages). Howard's next two Agnes stories would never reach the heights of the first: once he had understood he would never sell the series as it had been conceived, the Texan tried new angles, to no avail, and he simply stopped trying when he understood that in order to sell the series, he would have had to forego precisely what made it original. The bittersweet element here being that Moore, influenced by Howard's Conan tales, had created a female fantasy character and had sold her series to *Weird Tales*, preventing Howard from turning his series into a fantasy one as well. Howard was once again confined by the limits of the pulp market and the expectations of editors unwilling to push the boundaries of what was a very stereotypical market. In "Sword Woman," Howard tells us that anyone should be in a position to lead the life he or she wants to, whatever the social status or sex. A bit too daring. Interestingly enough, a few weeks after he completed "Sword Woman," he started dating Novalyne Price, a particularly strong-spirited young lady, who had no intentions of becoming a stay-at-home wife. Howard, who was in certain respects very much a man of his time and place as to the so-called "weaker sex," was soon confronted with his contradictions as to the status of women. A few months later, he would write "Red Nails," co-starring Conan and Valeria, about which more below.

16. "Beyond the Black River"

Written: circa August 1934.
First publication: *Weird Tales*, May and June 1935 (2-part serial).
Recommended modern edition: *The Conquering Sword of Conan*, Del Rey Books, 2005.

Synopsis: The king of Aquilonia will not listen to the pleas of his captains posted on the western outposts of his kingdom. They have noticed that the numerous Pictish tribes who live beyond the rivers that mark the end of civilization and the beginning of the wild, are acting in an increasingly menacing manner. The situation is even more alarming since, for the first time ever, the Picts have found in Zogar Sag a leader and a man able to unite under his name the various warring clans. Divided, the tribes were, at best, an episodic nuisance on a handful of habitations. United, they are a threat to the status quo. The story opens as Conan kills a Pict and thus saves the life of Balthus, a young settler fresh from the province of Tauran. On the other hand, he is too late for a second target, the merchant Tiberias, who had been indirectly responsible for the imprisonment of Zogar Sag. The shaman had managed to escape, swearing death for everyone who had contributed in one way or another to his capture. In the case of Tiberias, a swamp demon accomplished the grisly task and beheaded the merchant on Zogar Sag's behalf. The confrontation between the Picts and the Aquilonian settlers is about to become a full-scale uprising, at a time when the latter are ill-equipped, and the king refuses to send reinforcements.

Commentary: As is customary with Howard, one has to take what he had to say about the short story with a grain a salt. Thus, to August Derleth, he wrote: "I wanted to see if I could write an interesting Conan yarn without sex interest." A laconic description of this masterpiece if there ever was one. To Lovecraft, he explained: "In the Conan story I've attempted a new style and setting entirely—abandoned the exotic settings of lost cities, decaying civilizations, golden domes, marble palaces, silk-clad dancing girls, etc., and thrown my story against a background of forests and rivers, log cabins, frontier outposts, buckskin-clad settlers, and painted tribesmen." Which is more explicit, but doesn't do justice to the tale and what Howard was trying to achieve. It's quite logically to Novalyne Price, his girlfriend, that Howard would confide about his hopes for the story: "I sold Wright a yarn like that a few months ago... I'm damned surprised he took it. It's different from my other Conan yarns.... no sex... only men fighting against the savagery and bestiality about to engulf them... It's filled with the important little things of civilization, little things that make men think civilization's worth living and dying for." Price wrote in her diary: "He was excited about it because it was about this country and it sold! He had a honing to write more about this country, not an ordinary cowboy yarn, or a wild west shoot 'em up, though God knew this country was alive with yarns like that waiting to be written. But in his heart, he wanted to say more than that. He wanted to tell the simple story of this country and the hardships the settlers had suffered, pitted against a frightened, semi-barbaric people—the Indians, who were trying to hold on to a way of life and a country they loved."

Many critics consider "Beyond the Black River" the best of the Conan series and of Howard's career. Its final lines have become famous and are often used as the epitome of the Cimmerian's grim philosophy (though it is not Conan, but an unnamed woodsman who utters the words): "Barbarism is the natural state of mankind.... Civilization is unnatural. It is a whim of circumstance. And barbarism must always ultimately triumph."

All the characters who are not barbarians meet their doom in the tale: Tiberias the merchant, symbol of civilized opulence and arrogance, unwilling or unable to adjust his civilized ways to life on the Frontier. But even the woodsmen, born to civilization but having lived their lives on the frontier, cannot hope to prevail: "They were sons of civilization, reverted to a semi-barbarism. [Conan] was a barbarian of a thousand generations of barbarians. They had acquired stealth and craft, but he had been born to these things. He excelled them even in lithe economy of motion. They were wolves, but he was a tiger." The frontiersmen, Balthus, and Valannus die because of this, and Howard's genius was not to sacrifice his story for the sake of the usual conventions of the genre. Die those who have to die, survive those who can. Howard takes great pains to explain us that Conan has much more in common with the Picts—against whom he is fighting—than with the Aquilonians he is helping. This is highlighted by the Venarium episode related by Balthus, discussing a battle that took place years ago: "The Cimmerians swarmed over the walls.... The barbarians swept out of the hills in a ravening horde, without

"A hut wall buckled under the ram-like impact."

Beyond the Black River
By ROBERT E. HOWARD

'A thrilling novelette of the Picts and the wizard Zogar Sag—a startling weird saga of terrific adventures and dark magic

"Beyond the Black River" interior illustration.

warning, and stormed Venarium with such fury none could stand before them. Men, women and children were butchered. Venarium was reduced to a mass of charred ruins, as it is to this day." Conan's remark to this tragedy is as short as it is effective: "I was [there]. I was one of the horde that swarmed over the walls." In other words, Conan—and the Cimmerians—did exactly to the Aquilonians what the Picts are attempting to do in the course of the story. Conan is a Cimmerian, hence "as ferocious as the Picts, and much more intelligent," and this explains why he is going to survive.

Howard distances himself from his creation in that tale, where Conan becomes almost superhuman. He has the utmost confidence in himself, is often compared to a giant, his name already repeated over the council fires, and where he survives, every other character dies. It is, once again, a story where it is difficult for the reader to project himself into a character the pastiches and various adaptations keep describing as a "hero" (in the sense of role model, or character we'd like to be(come). Conan survives because he is the harshest, because he belongs to those who once slaughtered men, women and children during the sack of Venarium, because in a tale where the sympathetic characters are settlers, people who have a family, Conan declares: "I'm a mercenary. I sell my sword to the highest bidder. I never planted wheat and never will, so long as there are other harvests to be reaped with the sword." Conan survives because he is an elemental killer. Neither Balthus (behind whom the critics have long recognized Howard himself) nor us readers would ever survive an attack of Picts.

17. "Black Canaan"

Written: August and/or September 1934.
First publication: *Weird Tales*, Jun 1936.
Recommended modern edition: *The Horror Stories of Robert E. Howard*, Del Rey Books, 2008.

Synopsis: Kirby Buckner left his native Arkansas many years ago. But when he receives a message urging him to come back home, in Canaan, the land of his ancestors, where trouble is brewing, he doesn't hesitate for an instant. A mysterious individual known as Saul Stark, aided by an equally mysterious young woman, is fomenting an uprising against the white settlers. Stark is apparently gifted with supernatural powers. No sooner has Buckner arrived in the region that he falls under the hypnotic sway of the sexually alluring woman and becomes her puppet. Whatever she wants him to do, he will do.

Commentary: "Canaan" would probably never be included in a "Top 20 Howard stories" list written by an American critic, simply because the word "nigger" appears many times in the course of the story. The story is usually seen as a particularly racist one, though it is absolutely not. Dealing with sensitive and/or painful subject matter? Yes. Racist? Not at all. Certainly, all the white characters of the tale are hideous racists at worst, undefendable paternalists at best, but these story elements don't give us a single clue as to where Howard stood. It doesn't tell us that Howard was a racist, it doesn't tell us that he wasn't a racist either: it is only a tale in which Howard portrays racist characters, in a text written at the first person by a white male, and which takes place in the Deep South in the late nineteenth century. Most white characters in "Canaan" border on the imbecilic, to put it mildly, and seem devoid of any power of coherent thought. Canaan is an enclave, cut off from the exterior world, of maybe frozen in time. Only Kirby Buckner has more brains than his former friends, using the word "nigger" only when he talks to the other characters, never when he addresses the reader. As Howard himself wrote in a letter to Lovecraft discussing the real life character and settings that would later serve at the basis for "Black Canaan": "white folks little above the negro in civilization, and much more dangerous and aggressive."

The main theme of the story is not there. The relations between the whites and the blacks only furnish the background for the tale, and with the possible exception of Buckner (and not all the time at that); there are no characters to which the reader could project himself into. White/black, swamp/town, Canaan/outside world, earth/bogs; the tale is a study in duality and opposition. "Canaan" is on many points a journey back to the beginning—something readily apparent in the toponymy. Goshen, in the Bible, is the name given to the promised land of Canaan after the Exodus. The choice of the name owes nothing to chance. Howard stated that his tale was "laid in the real Canaan, which lies between Tulip Creek and the Ouachita River in southwestern Arkansaw, the homeland of the Howards." Isaac Howard, Bob Howard's father, was born and had spent the first fifteen years of his life in that region. "Canaan" is thus a journey back to where it all began, described in no uncertain terms as a mossy and wet triangle, and which would probably have given Sigmund Freud a field day. "Canaan" is thus the tale where the son comes back to the land which gave him birth, the exact counterpart to the Conan tales, in which the Cimmerian found his homeland so bleak and gloomy he left it forever. It should be now obvious that this is very far from exhausting the subject. "Canaan" is incredibly rich on the symbolic level, a dimension that has gone unseen and unexplored because of the smokescreen of the "race" question, whose function is precisely to hide what the story really deals with.

18. "Vultures of Wahpeton"

Written: September 1934.
First Publication: *Smashing Novels Magazine*, December 1936.
Recommended modern edition: *Grim Lands: The Best of Robert E. Howard Volume 2*, Del Rey Books, 2007.

Synopsis: John Middleton, sheriff of Wahpeton, arrives too late to save his deputy, Jim Grimes, shot down in cold blood in one of the town's saloons. He warns everyone that things are going to change sooner than later, and announces he has hired the services of a gunfighter from Texas, who will help him restore law and order. The next morning, two strangers meet in the hills nearby. They engage in conversation, apparently in a friendly manner, but the reader soon realizes that appearances are deceptive: both men know perfectly well who the other really is. They draw at the same moment, and one crumples to the ground, shot dead. John Middleton arrives at this precise moment. The dead man was the deadly gunfighter he had hired. Ever the pragmatist, he concludes that the newcomer, Corcoran, must be an ever better marksman, and he hires him on the sport to help clean the buzzard's nest that is Wahpeton. Corcoran is about to discover the situation in Wahpeton is much more complex than what Middleton hinted.

Commentary: Howard had the utmost difficulties selling "Vultures" to the pulp editors of the day. It very much seems it was the last tale he ever sold, in June 1936, after it had been circulated for more than a year and a half. The quality of the tale was very probably not the cause, but the angle Howard had adopted and the sheer originality of his treatment, twenty years ahead of anything that was appearing on the newsstands of the time. Howard probably felt he was going a bit too far and wrote two endings, the regular, logic and bitter one, and the convenient "happy end," far from convincing and which hurts considerably the impact and achievement of the tale.

In "Vultures," people are not who they seem to be. It is very tempting to read the tale as an expanded rewrite, in western guise, of

"The Shadow Kingdom," with its climate of rampant paranoia. Its writing was probably prompted by a revision job Howard had just completed, with a similar theme, incidentally titled "Vultures' Sanctuary," and markedly inferior to "Vultures". As if Howard had seen the potential of the tale and had written his own version as soon as he was done with the rewrite.

No one is truly white or black in "Wahpeton," in which the traditional values are reversed. The "good guys" wear the clothes of the bad ones, and vice versa. Impossible not to think of the first minutes of Sam Peckinpah's "The Wild Bunch" when reading the beginning of Howard's tale, both stories playing with the shock that comes from discovering the "heroes" are not who we thought they were, and that the function doesn't make the man. Almost entirely devoid of the clichés that plagued the genre, one only needs to have ready a handful of 1930s western magazines to fully realize the depth of the gap that separates Howard's text from the average pulp tale.

19. "Pigeons from Hell"

Written: November and/or December 1934.
First publication: *Weird Tales*, May 1938.
Recommended modern edition: *Grim Lands: The Best of Robert E. Howard Volume 2*, Del Rey Books, 2007.

Synopsis: Griswell awakes slowly. Remembers. He and his friend Branner, New Englanders both, took refuge for the night in an old deserted manor house somewhere in the South. They slept on the planks of the ground floor. Griswell had an agitated sleep. As his eyes slowly get accustomed to the dark, he remembers it was a noise that woke him up. He distinguishes the figure of his friend, slowly walking down the steps from the second floor, an axe stuck in his skull, obviously dead.

Commentary: The title "Pigeons from Hell" is, from a modern viewpoint, far from a terrifying one (except perhaps to those readers who live in metropolitan areas invaded by said creatures), but for an American reader from the ex-Confederate States living in the aftermath of the Secession War and/or during the Reconstruction, it would have been more than disquieting.

"Pigeons from Hell" interior illustration by Virgil Finlay in the May 1938 issue of Weird Tales.

In September 1930, Howard, who had just initiated what would become the major correspondence of his life, with H.P. Lovecraft, explained: "As regards African-legend sources, I well remember the tales I listened to and shivered at, when a child in the 'piney woods' of East Texas, where Red River marks the Arkansaw and Texas boundaries. There were quite a number of old slave darkies still living then. The one to whom I listened most was the cook, old Aunt Mary Bohannon.... Aunt Mary said that when a good spirit passes, a breath of cool air follows; but when an evil spirit goes by a blast from the open doors of Hell follows it.... Another tale she told that I have often met with in negro-lore. The setting, time and circumstances are changed by telling, but the tale remains basically the same. Two or three men—usually Negroes—are travelling in a wagon through some isolated district—usually a broad, deserted river-bottom. They come on to the ruins of a once thriving plantation at dusk, and decideto spend the night in the deserted plantation house. This house is always huge, brooding and forbidding, and always, as the men approach the high columned verandah, through the high weeds that surround the house, great numbers of pigeons rise from their roosting places on the railing and fly away. The men sleep in the big front-room with its crumbling fire-place, and in the night they are awakened by a jangling of chains, weird noises and groans from upstairs. Sometimes footsteps descend the stairs with no visible cause. Then a terrible apparition appears to the men who flee in terror. This monster, in all the tales I have heard, is invariably a headless giant, naked or clad in a shapeless sort of garment, and is sometimes armed with a broad-axe. This motif appears over and over in negro-lore.... But through most of the stories I heard in my childhood, the dark, brooding old plantation house loomed as a horrific back-ground and the human or semi-human horror, with its severed head was woven in the fiber of the myths."

"Pigeons from Hell" is not just a horror tale; it is specifically a horror tale of the American South. It is also (as critic Brian Leno has conclusively shown) very much a reaction to, and an attack on, H.P. Lovecraft, who had explained that New England—Lovecrafts's native region—was "the" perfect background for a horror tale. With "Pigeons," Howard demonstrates the absurdity of Lovecraft's claim, and insidiously takes shots at his Providence colleague, in a clear echo of the often virulent exchanges of their letters by that time. That the two travellers are New Englanders is of course no coincidence, no more than the title of some chapters—"The Whistler in the Dark" or "The Call of the Zuvembie," echoing Lovecraft's "The Whisperer in the Dark" and "The Call of Cthulhu." Griswell seems unable to react to what is happening to him other than by fleeing, fainting and feeling nauseous, in typical Lovecraftian protagonist fashion. The attitude of Buckner, the no-nonsense local sheriff, makes for a striking contrast. Even if he has a hard time believing Griswell at first, he was born and bred in the region and is thus perfectly aware of the occasional manifestations of the supernatural in the area. When his torchlight gives up on him, it is not so much the unexplainable mystery surrounding the occurrence which makes him pause, but the consequences this may have on his and Griswell's safety. Buckner is the character who firmly roots the horror from the past of the story in the contemporary world the characters evolve in. The isolated and deserted house of the tale shares many common points with other isolated or remote places in Howard's fiction, such as the enclave of "Black Canaan" and the city of Xuchotl in "Red Nails," places that are often privileged settings for horror.

Howard takes pains never to reveal the exact location of the tale, thus giving his narrative a wider scope than Canaan and a certain allegorical level. "Pigeons" is about horror in the southern portion of the USA, by which one should understand the ex-Confederate states. On a wider scale, "Pigeons" is a superb allegory of the decay of the Southern "aristocracy" on the heels of the Secession War, an era which belongs to the past of the protagonists, but where the ghosts—or rather the zuvembies—still haunt the region decades later, reminders of the sinister heritage of an era where wealth, elegance and pride often concealed the atrocities perpetrated on the slaves. Howard's sympathies in that tale are clearly with the mulatto woman, badly mistreated by her mistress, and who will enact her fearsome vengeance without being captured or punished.

> *Howard often declared that the slaves on his ancestors' "plantations" (an exaggeration) were never mistreated or badly used. He was probably unaware of the exactions of his great-grandfather Henry Howard, whose father-in-law's will read: "I am of the opinion that slaves & negroes should be treated with humanity, therefore my will and desire is that none of my negroes should fall into the hands of Henry Howard." It very much seems there were zuvembies hidden in Howard's ancestry.*

20. "Red Nails"

Written: late June and July 1935.
First publication: *Weird Tales*, August, September/October and November 1936 (3-part serial).
Recommended modern edition: *The Conquering Sword of Conan*, Del Rey Books, 2005.

Synopsis: Conan eventually catches up with Valeria of the Red Brotherhood after a long chase. The young woman had to flee the town of Sukhmet after killing an insistent Stygian officer who had made advances to her. Valeria is not particularly impressed with Conan, having understood perfectly well what the Cimmerian was interested in: "a stallion could have made it no plainer," she tells him. As they are engaged in a lively discussion, they are set upon by a Hyborian Age "dragon" (almost always illustrated as a stegosaurus even though the description is clearly that of a spinosaurus). After a frightful fight, Conan and Valeria barely escape with their lives, having no idea they have just slain the last of the beasts that used to roam the region surrounding the city they soon discover in the distance. They will soon discover that the city is a very peculiar one indeed, entirely walled, paved, roofed and devoid of windows. Xuchotl—they will later learn its name—is literally cut off from the exterior world. It doesn't take long for them to stumble upon the first inhabitant of the town.

Commentary: In the spring of 1935, Howard declared that he was about to write yet another Conan story, while he was perfectly aware that *Weird Tales* was on shaky financial grounds and thus that it would takes months, perhaps years, before he would get any payment. The tale had been germinating for quite a long time, as he was already mentioning certain aspects of the story in conversations he had with Novalyne Price in December 1934, but the actual writing phase only began after he visited Lincoln, New Mexico, where had occurred the Bloody Lincoln County War. It was there that he found the last elements he needed, and that the story "jelled"—as he had it. His detailed explanation to Lovecraft is worth reading, giving precious clues as to what he was doing with that Conan tale:

"Lincoln is a haunted place; it is a dead town; yet it lives with a life that died fifty years ago.... I have never felt anywhere the exact sensations Lincoln aroused in me—a sort of horror predominating. If there is a haunted spot on this hemisphere, then Lincoln is haunted.... [Y]et it is not merely the fact of knowing so many men died there that makes it haunted, to me.... The valley in which Lincoln lies is isolated from the rest of the world. Vast expanses of desert and mountains separate it from the rest of humanity—deserts too barren to support human life. The people in Lincoln lost touch with the world. Isolated as they were, their own affairs, their relationship with

> *"When I learned of Robert Howard's death, I was very upset. I came into the offices one day and Wright informed me of Howard's suicide. We both just sat around and cried for most of the day. He was always my personal favorite"*
>
> — *Margaret Brundage*

one another, took on an importance and significance out of proportion to their actual meaning. Thrown together too much, jealousies and resentments rankled and grew, feeding upon themselves, until they reached monstrous proportions and culminated in those bloody atrocities which startled even the tough West of that day.... In such restricted, isolated spots, human passions smolder and burn, feeding on the impulses which give them birth, until they reached a point that can hardly be conceived by dwellers in more fortunate spots.... I have heard of people going mad in isolated places; I believe the Lincoln County War was tinged with madness."

"Red Nails" is the counterpart to "Beyond the Black River," in which Howard stated that "Civilization is unnatural." "Red Nails" was the story in which he would expand on that theme. In all the stories he had written on the subject, the decadent and decaying phase of his civilizations, kingdoms, countries, or cities was never allowed to be carried out in its entirety: once divided and thus weakened, the civilized people were systematically wiped out by hordes of barbarians (conveniently) waiting at the gates. "Red Nails" is different in the sense that no tribe of barbarians is lurking at the gates of Xuchotl. For the first time in Howard's fiction, the civilizing process, with its decadent and decaying phases, is carried out to its inevitable end. Xuchotl is an "unnatural" city in the sense implied in "Beyond the Black River": to be civilized is to be entirely removed from nature and its forces. This is the reason why the city is not only cut off from the rest of the Hyborian world and its barbarian tribes, it is also, and equally importantly, cut off from nature itself. Xuchotl is the epitome of a decayed civilization as Howard conceived it. It is the place where, as he had it, "the abnormal becomes normal."

A lot could be said about the relationship between Conan and Valeria, for instance, in which it is quite tempting to see a parallel with that of Howard and Novalyne Price. Tascela, the female vampire who refuses to die, feeding on younger women, fighting for the attentions of Conan, and thus jealous of Valeria, could very well be a fictional representation of Howard's mother, who was always hostile toward Novalyne Price. Olmec would thus be seen as Howard's father, and the whole story an allegorical tale, in which Howard and Novalyne Price set foot in the decayed universe that has become the Howard house in 1935, where Howard's mother would linger one more year before her death.

"If somebody asks you where you get your characters... and they're sure to do that... you always say, 'He's a combination of a lot of people I have known.' That way, if your character is a damn fool, nobody will want to identify with him... To tell the truth, I don't know how a man gets a character for a story, anymore than I know how he falls in love. I don't know if his characters spring full-blown from his head, or if he sees a man walking down the street and recognizes him instantly... I doubt any writer knows for sure where his characters come from."

– Robert E. Howard

Chapter Four
Twenty More Tales You Should Read

1. "Nekht Semerkeht" (originally untitled)

Written: probably in May and/or June 1936. Unfinished.
Recommended modern edition: *The Black Stranger and Other American Tales*, Bison Books, 2005.

Synopsis: America, 16th century. Hernando de Guzman wanders in the immensities of the desert. His horse has just died on him, and his end seems near. He is haunted by the prospect of his own mortality, and ponders on the need to keep on fighting just to survive. The deep booming of a drum in the distance brings him back to reality...

Commentary: It was very probably his suicide that prevented Howard from completing the text. He seems to allude to it in a letter written a few weeks before his death. What has come to us is a fascinating and tantalizing—though unfinished—tale, half-western, half-weird tale, punctuated with incongruous and frankly disturbing erotic passages and with a series of philosophical reflections on the futility of human existence. What would have been, under other circumstances, an odd tale at most, takes a strange resonance when put against the background of Howard's impending suicide.

2. "Sharp's Gun Serenade"

Written: 1936.
First publication: *Action Stories*, January 1937.
Recommended modern edition: *Crimson Shadows: The Best of Robert E. Howard Volume 1*, Del Rey Books, 2007.

Synopsis: Breckinridge Elkins finds a haggard Jack Sprague, rope in hand. A short while later, he encounters a second individual who asks if he has seen Sprague; the matter is pressing, as the newcomer explains that Sprague has had suicidal tendencies since his fiancée dumped him in favor of another man…

Commentary: This Breckinridge Elkins tale is the rewrite of a prior version of the story (titled "Educate or Bust,") which Howard had written specifically for the British market. As his writing time was seriously dwindling in the early part of 1936, he decided to recycle the basic frame of the story and to sell the result to *Action Stories*, the pulp magazine in which the series was running. Howard introduced quite a number of changes, though, most notably the character of Jack Sprague (and his suicidal leanings). At the end of the story, Sprague will get over his pain by falling in love and eloping with the schoolmistress of the region, the one on which Breck had set his sights. The tale takes particular resonance when we remember that Howard had just put an end to his love affair with Novalyne Price, herself a teacher. Difficult also not to be moved by the following paragraph in the story: "When a man is in his state he ain't responsible and it's the duty of his friends to look after him. He'll thank us in the days to come."

3. "Black Colossus"

Written: circa September and October 1932.
First publication: *Weird Tales*, June 1933.
Recommended modern edition: *The Coming of Conan the Cimmerian*, Del Rey Books, 2003.

Synopsis: A wind of revolt blows from the mysterious city-states of the southern regions of the Hyborian world. Natohk, a mysterious veiled sorcerer, walks North and nothing can stop his hosts. He desires the Princess Yasmela, who is sister to the King of Khoraja. In dreams Natohk tells her he is coming to make her his bride. Desperate, she seeks advice from the gods. The oracle from Mitra tells her to give command of her armies to the first man she meets in the street. Going out, she stumbles upon Conan.

Commentary: "Black Colossus" is the first Conan tale slanted toward an easy sale and grabbing the cover spot… which succeeded perfectly. Howard, who had been writing tale after tale about the Cimmerian for many months, was realizing, in these lean times, that Conan could be an easy meal-ticket. It is thus not surprising to see that he was distancing himself a bit from the Cimmerian, writing to his friend Tevis Clyde Smith: "My heroes grow more bastardly as the years pass. One of my latest sales concluded with a sexual intercourse instead of the usual slaughter. My sword-wielder grabbed the princess—already considerably stripped by the villing [sic]—and smacked her down on the altar of the forgotten gods, while battle and massacre roared outside, and through the dusk the remains of the villing, nailed to the wall by the hero, regarded the pastime sardonically. I don't know how the readers will like it. I'll bet some of them will. The average man has a secret desire to be a swaggering, drunken, fighting, raping swashbuckler." "Black Colossus" has its share of unconvincing scenes, but also of excellent writing. What can one say about the tale's introductory chapter, which is nothing short of brilliant? In a few sentences, Howard makes Shevatas come alive and establishes an oppressive atmosphere with impressive skill.

4. "People of the Black Coast"

Written: 1928, probably second trimester.
First publication: *Spaceway Science Fiction*, September/October 1969.
Recommended modern edition: *Adventures in Science-Fantasy*, REH Foundation Press, 2012

Synopsis: The protagonist and Gloria, his female companion, find themselves stranded on the shores of an uncharted isle surrounded by a series of unscalable basaltic cliffs which prevent them from getting inland.

Commentary: The world is divided into two categories: those who hate this story, and those who love it. The tale has all the earmarks of a feverish nightmare and is hypnotic in its intensity. The scene in which the hero leaves his companion for a while before coming back to her and stumbles on a particularly grisly sight will stay with you.

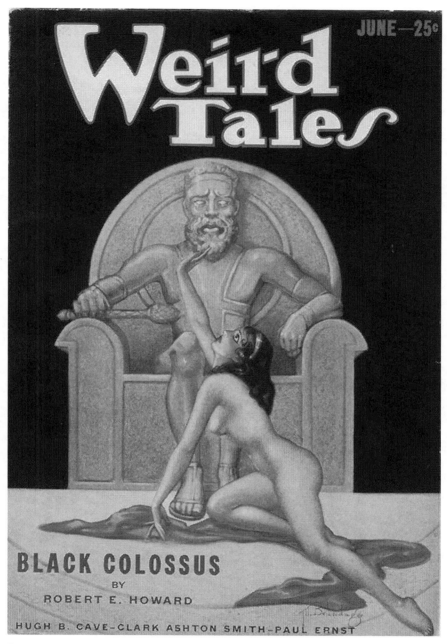

June 1933 Weird Tales *with "Black Colossus" cover by Brundage.*

5. "Spear and Fang"

Written: circa October 1924.
First publication: *Weird Tales*, July 1925.
Recommended modern edition: *Shadow Kingdoms*, Wildside Press, 2005.

Synopsis: The young A-aea is in love with Ga-Nor, a Cro-Magnon man with artistic inclinations, but Ka-nanu has every intention to separate the young lovers. A Neanderthal man, a primitive belonging to that species of child devourers, or at least that's what people say, kidnaps her. Ga-Nor understands what happened and decides to rescue the young woman.

Commentary: This was Howard's first professional sale, absolutely devoid of any weird or fantasy element, as it clearly belongs to the then-thriving tradition of prehistoric stories. While there is not much to say to defend the literary qualities of this juvenile production, it is particularly important to note that Howard began his career in a magazine devoted to the weird and the horrific with a proto-historical tale.

6. "Kings of the Night"

Written: circa March 1930.
First publication: *Weird Tales*, November 1930.
Recommended modern edition: *Kull: Exile of Atlantis*, Del Rey Books, 2006.

Synopsis: Bran Mak Morn, king of the fast-waning Pictish nation, finds himself in a delicate situation. The alliance between his own Pictish tribes, members of various Gaelic warriors and a troop of Norsemen is particularly shaky, and he greatly fears that the frail unity will break before the battle that will pit them against the Roman legions. And his fears are justified when the Norsemen inform him they won't follow him unless he can find them a king they can trust to lead them to battle, an impossible task.

Commentary: "Kings of the Night" enabled Howard to team up Bran and Kull the Atlantean, in a tale that would be his farewell to the latter character. Much can be said as to the story being a symbolic enactment of a transmission: Howard's previous (and first) royal character, Kull of Atlantis, having become an autocratic ruler in the last tales of his own cycle, is here portrayed as a carefree character, content only in the blind happy madness of battle, while Bran (whom Howard described as a chief in previous tales) has now become a king, but a king on whom the crown lies heavy, burdened as he is by the fate of his people and the loyalty that gives meaning to his way of life, in a tale where he has no choice but to sacrifice some of his allies to save his nation.

7.   Hawk of the Hills

Written: probably late 1934.
First publication: *Top-Notch*, June 1935.
Recommended modern edition: *Crimson Shadows: The Best of Robert E. Howard Volume 1*, Del Rey Books, 2007.

Synopsis: A tribal war in the Afghan hills has been going on for nearly three years. Britain decides it is time to act on the problem and sends one of its best men in the region, Willoughby, with a simple mission: to restore peace.

Commentary: By far the best story starring Francis Xavier Gordon, aka "El Borak" (the Swift). The character was a definitely pulpish creation, owing something to Talbot Mundy's Athelstan King. Most of the El Borak tales make for a pleasant read, but this one is several notches above the rest, providing Howard with the perfect spot to reflect with a striking lucidity on the question of colonialism and imperialism (the British one, in this case), the hypocrisy that necessarily goes along with it, the blindness of those same occidental powers to the unavoidable consequences their blundering actions have on the indigenous populations, and their national and international repercussions

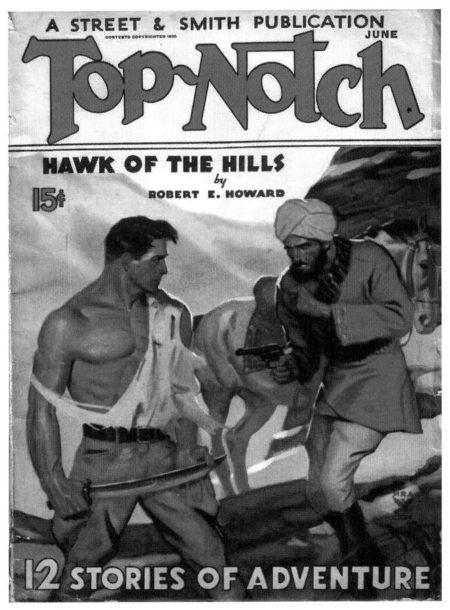

June 1935 issue of Top-Notch *with "Hawk of the Hills" cover.*

Pure pulpish fare with a message to deliver, as powerful today as it was eighty years ago, and a perfect example of Howard's lucidity and visionary accomplishments.

8. "The Grey God Passes"

Written: December 1931.
First publication: *Dark Mind, Dark Heart*, edited by August Derleth, Arkham House, 1962.
Recommended modern edition: *Crimson Shadows: The Best of Robert E. Howard Volume 1*, Del Rey Books, 2007.

Synopsis: The battle of Clontarf, which opposed the Celtic forces of King Brian Boru to the Nordic invaders on the plains near Dublin in 1014, with Odin, the grey god himself, as a guest star.

Commentary: Here is a tale that will never make it to anyone's "best of" list because of the sheer number of characters Howard uses, which makes for a sometimes very difficult reading, unless one is readily extremely familiar with the events depicted. This being said, the tale's first chapter, its sumptuous finale, and the idea to make of this battle the literal Ragnarok of the Norse in Ireland... are just too great not to mention. To mix to such a degree the epic and the historical in a particularly inspired and poetic style is an exploit, even if an imperfect one.

9. "Rogues in the House"

Written: December 1932 or January 1933.
First publication: *Weird Tales*, January 1934.
Recommended modern edition: *The Coming of Conan the Cimmerian*, Del Rey Books, 2003.

Synopsis: Murilo, a young aristocrat, is an opponent to Nabonidus, a.k.a. the Red Priest, whom many think is the real ruler of the city. When the priest makes it clear to Murilo that he is his next target, the nobleman goes to the city prison to find one he hopes can help him defeat his foe. He stumbles upon a Cimmerian, jailed after having been betrayed by his companion, a woman of ill-repute. Murilo offers him his freedom in exchange for the elimination of the priest. The Cimmerian readily agrees.

Commentary: Damon Knight was particularly impressed by the scene of Conan dumping the traitress in a cesspool. Granted. But the tale is first and foremost a fascinating exploration of the question of evolution, then a burning issue. Is Thak an ape-man or a man-ape? Is he the reflection we don't want to stare at? Our past or our future? Howard puts the reader face to face with his own fears: Darwin had dealt a terrible blow to the religious conception of the origins of mankind. The Great Monkey trial of 1925 was a recent and painful reminder of the question, as was, in many ways, the disproportionate percentage of giant apes and gorillas in the popular arts of the first half of twentieth century America. To the "anthropological anxiety" (which is what Howard's tale mainly deals with) was coupled a more diffuse sexual anxiety, because of the more or less unconscious violently racist link established between the African-Americans and the great apes. One only has to reread Lovecraft's "Arthur Jermyn," Henry S. Whitehead's "Williamson" or watch again *King Kong* (1933) to realize the potent sexual theme driving those tales. Howard's tale is much tamer in that respect and deals mostly with the anthropological aspects of the question. "Rogues in the House" is a locked room mystery, in which every wall is a mirror, forcing the reader to confront his own truth.

10. "Wings in the Night"

Written: Spring 1930.
First publication: *Weird Tales*, July 1932.
Recommended modern edition: *The Savage Tales of Solomon Kane*, Del Rey Books, 2004.

Synopsis: Solomon Kane stumbles upon a horrific scene: a whole African village reduced to ruins, all its inhabitants slaughtered. Amidst all this horror, a peculiar detail strikes the Puritan: there are bodies in the trees. He finds a lone survivor, delirious and nearing death. The man hast just the time to mumble something about wings before dying. Kane makes his way to a second village, where the tribe welcomes him as a friend. It is there that he will get to learn what happened in the first village.

Commentary: While Howard never could match the intensity of the first Solomon Kane story, he did produce a few memorable tales about the Puritan. "Wings in the Night" is probably the best of those, playing as it does on the madness of Kane. Impossible not to think about Hamlet when Kane soliloquizes to the severed head which has become his privileged companion all the while he patiently elaborates his vengeance: "Kane toiled by day and by night, and between his stints he talked to the shriveled, mummied head of Goru, whose eyes, strangely enough, did not change in the blaze of the sun or the haunt of the moon, but retained their life-like expression. When the memory of those lunacy-haunted days had become only a vague nightmare, Kane wondered if, as it had seemed to him, Goru's dried lips had moved in answer, speaking strange and mysterious things." The tale has a few shortcomings, but its main interests reside in its ideas (the mythological background) and memorable scenes (Kane's near-madness.)

11. The Hour of the Dragon

Written: from mid-March 1934 to mid-May 1934.
First publication: *Weird Tales*, December 1935, January, February, March and April 1936 (serial).
Recommended modern edition: *The Conquering Sword of Conan*, Del Rey Books, 2005

<u>Synopsis</u>: Four conspirators resurrect the mummy of Xaltotun, a sorcerer who lived three thousand years before. Their objective is simple: to use the esoteric knowledge of the dead sorcerer to win the war that will oppose them to Conan, king of Aquilonia, a country they devoutly wish to annex to their empire. However, the schemers have neglected to take into account Xaltotun's own aspirations and his power, as well as that of the Heart of Ahriman, the mystic jewel they used to resurrect him.

Commentary: The only novel starring Conan. The book with which Howard had decided to crash the British market, though this wasn't to be. A book which, had it been published, would have changed the history of fantasy as we know it. The facts are known: in 1933, Howard submitted a collection of his best tales to a British publisher who had shown definite interest in his work. After many weeks, the collection was refused on the grounds that there was a prejudice in England against short stories, and encouraging Howard to submit a full-length novel "on the same order". Undaunted, Howard complied with the request, even if he had no real assurance it would sell. Unfortunately, the British publisher ran into financial difficulties a few weeks afterward and the novel was returned.

The Hour of the Dragon is a perfect example of what Raymond Chandler called a "cannibalization," a novel recycling several elements from anterior short stories. The British readership wouldn't have been familiar with the short stories published in an American magazine. For the first and last time of his career, Howard used the motif of the quest as the backbone of his story, visibly patterned after the Arthurian legend (which was logical, given the—intended— readership.)

The Hour of the Dragon has moments of real excellence, most notably in its first and last parts. A few chapters are exhilarating, the prime examples being the passage in which Conan takes control of the pirate ship, exceptionally well written, and Conan's triumphant return to Aquilonia. The Cimmerian's considerations on the royal function and its implications are striking. Howard masterfully describes scenes of war on an epic scale, but devotes equal attention to the consequences of war and occupation on the common people. This being said, the novel is not without structural difficulties, as Howard had not fully mastered the art of writing such long works, and some portions of the middle section are not particularly useful. Though half-successful in some respects, the historical importance of *The Hour of the Dragon* should not be denied.

12. The Mirrors of Tuzun Thune

Written: September or October 1927.
First publication: *Weird Tales*, September 1929.
Recommended modern edition: *Kull: Exile of Atlantis*, Del Rey Books, 2006.

Synopsis: Kull has been neglecting his royal duties since he met the mysterious Tuzun Thune, who invited him to come to his place to gaze into his various and intriguing mirrors.

Commentary: "The Mirrors of Tuzun Thune" is one of Howard's most poetical texts, less a story than a series of philosophical musings on power, reality and illusion. One of those texts that deserve to be read rather than analyzed...

12. "The Moon of Skulls"

Written: circa March 1929.
First publication: *Weird Tales*, June and July 1930 (serial).
Recommended modern edition: *The Savage Tales of Solomon Kane*, Del Rey Books, 2004.

Synopsis: "The Moon of Skulls" tells the story of a man, Solomon Kane, who traveled thousands of miles, from Europe to Africa, in a quest that lasted years, to save a young woman.

Commentary: One needs only replace "save" with "avenge" to see that "The Moon of Skulls" is essentially another take on the basic framework of "Red Shadows," the first Solomon Kane story, expanded and updated. One of the most interesting features of this new version is the replacing of "Le Loup" by the queen of Negari, two disreputable characters who take great pleasure in inflicting pain to young women and raping them. The vampire-queen's lesbianism is of course never openly stated in the course of the tale, but one would be blind not to see what is really going in the scenes between her and Marylin, the young girl. Nakari of Negari is Kane's opposite: where she is black of skin (her name and country are transparent enough), his has a cadaveric pallor, and the first letters of her name are those of the Puritan, spelled backwards. One can readily understand the strange fascination to which both characters succumb to as soon as they are in presence of the other, drawn to / repulsed by their doppelgänger, fighting to protect / defame innocence (embodied here in Marylin). Lilith, as Kane calls Nakari, is an apt equivalent, as she is the woman of the night, symbol of sexuality as well of infertility. She is the woman that lures men to their doom. Given what we wrote before as to Howard's carnal appetites, it is far from certain that the Texan would have manifested the same steely resolve as his Puritan righter of wrongs...

Weird Tales *June 1930 with "Moon of Skulls" cover by Hugh Rankin.*

13. "Mountain Man"

Written: between 16 and 30 June 1933.
First publication: *Action Stories*, March/April 1934.
Recommended modern edition: *The Adventures of Breckinridge Elkins*, volume 1, REH Foundation Press, 2016.

Synopsis: The first Breckinridge Elkins of Bear Creek tale, starring the most improbable hero, as unreliable a narrator as Steve Costigan, Howard's sailor and boxer. As the story opens, Breck's father asks him to go to the village of Tomahawk to fetch a letter. Breck gets ready to leave the family nest for the first time ever and to discover "civilization" in the process.

Commentary: The Breckinridge Elkins series was one of Howard's most important commercial success. All the tales in the series are replete with hilarious passages, showcasing Howard's talent and ear for idiomatic "langwidge". If the opening paragraphs of the tale don't convince you, you don't need read any of the tales.

I was robbing a bee tree, when I heard my old man calling: "Breckinridge! Oh, Breckinridge! Where air you? I see you now. You don't need to climb that tree. I ain't goin' to larrup you."

He come up, and said: "Breckinridge, ain't that a bee settin' on yore ear?"

I reached up, and sure enough, it was. Come to think about it, I had felt kind of like something was stinging me somewhere.

"I swan, Breckinridge," said pap, "I never seen a hide like your'n. Listen to me: old Buffalo Rogers is back from Tomahawk, and the postmaster there said they was a letter for me, from Mississippi. He wouldn't give it to nobody but me or some of my folks. I dunno who'd be writin' me from Mississippi; last time I was there, was when I was fightin' the Yankees. But anyway, that letter is got to be got. Me and yore maw has decided you're to go git it. Yuh hear me, Breckinridge?"

"Clean to Tomahawk?" I said. "Gee whiz, pap!"

The Sailor Steve Costigan tales were in the same vein, but many suffer from the restrictions imposed on them by the need to have a boxing fight in each and every story. Free from such a burden, Howard could let his imagination run wild in the Breckinridge Elkins tales, and wild it ran! Given their style and peculiar humor, these "short stories and tall tales" deserve an audio edition!

14. "A Witch Shall be Born"

Written: June 1934.
First publication: *Weird Tales*, December 1934.
Recommended modern edition: *The Bloody Crown of Conan*, Del Rey Books, 2004.

Synopsis: Queen Taramis of Khauran is awakened by an apparition. Soon enough, she discovers that the spectral intruder is a woman, who reveals herself as her twin sister, Salome, nicknamed the witch, who was supposed to have been killed soon after her birth. Salome then proceeds to explain her sister that she will usurp her identity and reign in her name, with her ally and general, the depraved general Constantius.

Commentary: Difficult to begin somewhere with this story. It is one of the most famous Conan tales because of the crucifixion scene: Conan, crucified, left to die in the desert, grabbing with his teeth the vulture which was preying on him, breaking the neck of the animal and quenching his thirst with its blood. Conan nailed to a cross made (and still makes) for a powerful image, especially so in a Christian country. The tale ends with an homage to Lovecraft with the monster of the final chapter, unless it was a cheap expedient to conclude it in a desultory manner, now that Howard had told the story he wanted to tell. The story is yet another illustration of Howard's obsession with the theme of the lost brother or sister (as in "People of the Black Circle", for instance). It was also the occasion for Margaret Brundage to deliver a superb cover illustration (from which the Cimmerian is noteworthily absent, as was almost always the rule). But when all is said and done, what one should remember from this text is the incredible modernity of its construction. Multiple viewpoints, kaleidoscopic narration, behind the scene action. Howard lets the reader fill many of the salient points of the story. Any second-rate writer would have written a full-length novel about Conan's slow ascension to power among the nomadic warriors. Howard spares us all these pages, which we have already anticipated and visualized in our mind's eye. It was particularly audacious in 1934. It still is.

15. "The Dark Man"

Written: early February 1930.
First publication: *Weird Tales*, December 1931.
Recommended modern edition: *Crimson Shadows: The Best of Robert E. Howard Volume 1*, Del Rey Books, 2007.

Synopsis: Ireland, soon after the battle of Clontarf (1014). Moira has been kidnapped by a Nordic pirate. Turlogh O'Brien, the Gaelic exile, goes after him in a desperate attempt to save the young woman. On his way, he finds an intriguing statue, having no idea it is a representation of the last king of the Pictish nation, Bran Mak Morn.

Commentary: The first Turlogh O'Brien tale, one of Howard's most fascinating characters, an "Irish outlaw whose adventures are laid in the half century preceding the battle of Hastings." One of the Texan's first success at combining in a single story all the themes he was obsessed with: the outcast, the woman who has to suffer because of men's desires and brutality, and whose only way of escape are either submission or suicide, the Gaelic civilization, the Picts, the futility of human endeavors… all this in a marvelously poetic prose.

16. "The Gods of Bal-Sagoth"

Written: circa April 1930.
First publication: *Weird Tales*, October 1931.
Recommended modern edition: *Swords of the North*, REH Foundation Press, 2014.

Synopsis: The sequel to "The Dark Man" (though published before in the pages of *Weird Tales*). Turlogh and Athelstane the Saxon find themselves stranded upon the shores of a mysterious island and attacked by a prehistoric beast. Soon after, they are caught in the power plays of Brunhilde, former—ruthless—ruler of the weird city she calls Bal-Sagoth. An ancient prophecy mentioning two men of steel coming from the sea, she decides to use them to take control of Bal-Sagoth again.

Commentary: "Bal-Sagoth" clearly announces the future masterpiece "Red Nails" with its two protagonists somewhat at odds with each other stumbling upon an isolated city where the inhabitants are at war against each other. The first chapter, as often with Howard, is brilliant, and the tale moves at breakneck speed, demonstrating, once again Howard's mastery at storytelling: it is only after the conclusion that we realize the twenty-pager contains a shipwreck, a supposedly extinct prehistoric beast, a coup d'état, an invasion from hordes of savages and an earthquake, leaving Jack Bauer a distant second in his efforts to catch up with Howard's protagonist!

18. "Wild Water"

Written: May or June 1933.
First publication: *Cross Plains* #7, George Hamilton, 1975.
Recommended modern edition: *Grim Lands: The Best of Robert E. Howard Volume 2*, Del Rey Books, 2007.

Synopsis: Saul Hopkins is the capitalistic king of the town of Bisley and its surroundings, lording it on everyone and imposing harsh conditions on impoverished farmers whose lives are but an endless series of sufferings. One man has had enough and decides it is time to take down Hopkins in old-fashion style: with a bullet in his heart.

Commentary: "Wild Water" is one of the very first westerns written by Howard. He sent it to his agent, who immediately warned him that, though he liked the tale, he would have a hard time selling it, which turned out to be prophetic. This western takes place, not in the nineteenth century, but in contemporary times. No cowboys and Indians, but poor tenant farmers. Reynolds, the gunfighter, is an anachronism in this modern world, where Hopkins rules undisputed, not even able to imagine he could be physically threatened, much less killed with a gun. The most unbelievable aspect of the tale—the filling of the lake in a matter of hours instead of three hours—is actually the one that is closest to reality: scientists had predicted it would take two years to fill Lake Brownwood, close to where Howard lived. It took only a particularly violent storm and six hours, in 1932, and it was evidently this event which furnished the background for "Wild Water."

The story is dense, harsh, much more morally complex than the synopsis would let one believe, and particularly well crafted. Howard leads his reader where he wants him to go, and it takes a while before we realize we should question our initial reactions, thanks to an excellent construction. So original, in fact, that there was no way the tale could have sold in the thirties.

19. "The Valley of the Worm"

Written: circa June 1932.
First publication: *Weird Tales*, February 1934.
Recommended modern edition: *Crimson Shadows: The Best of Robert E. Howard Volume 1*, Del Rey Books, 2007.

Synopsis: Texan James Allison is a cripple, awaiting death, "which creeps slowly on him like a blind slug." What he is most bitter about is not so much his fate than the drabness of his existence, so unlike his forebears who all led full and colorful lives. His only compensation, a recently acquired capacity, is his ability to remember his past lives, especially those of times as distant as they were heroic.

Commentary: The most famous of the tales starring James Allison. The series found its origins in the fascination Howard had for reincarnation, and its form in his love for Jack London's *The Star Rover*, in which prisoner Darrell Standing's only solace from his life in a cell is his ability to remember his past lives. The three stories starring Allison, or, to be more precise, three of his past incarnations, are the onlyones in Howard's career in which the major character is a Nordic barbarian (clearly derived from London's Ragnar Lodbrog). Howard's barbarians of choice were almost always Gaelic (or pseudo-Gaelic) or Pictish, but never Nordic. Niord, the blonde-haired "Aryan" (i.e. Indo-European) powerhouse, is anything but a typical Howard hero. In a few tales where Howard portrayed seemingly invincible warriors, he

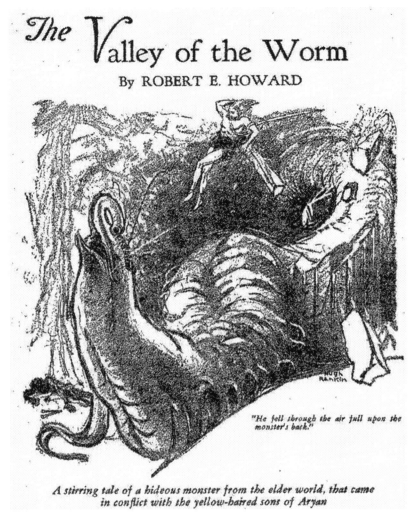

The Valley of the Worm

By ROBERT E. HOWARD

"He fell through the air full upon the monster's back."

A stirring tale of a hideous monster from the elder world, that came in conflict with the yellow-haired sons of Aryan

"The Valley of the Worm" interior illustration by Hugh Rankin.

would always—unconsciously?—create a weaker character, behind whom it's easy to recognize Howard himself. The most famous example of this process being the young settler Balthus in "Beyond the Black River," in which Conan is portrayed as a true killing machine. It is difficult not to see in the miserable James Allison, chained to his house in the post-oak country of central Texas, a reflection of Howard himself, and the same goes for Grom, a typical Howard Pict.

20. "The Night of the Wolf"

Written: May 1930.
First publication: *Bran Mak Morn*, Dell Books, 1969.
Recommended modern edition: *Swords of the North*, REH Foundation Press, 2014.

Synopsis: A mysterious individual named Partha McOthna appears at the *skalli* of the Viking warriors. No one seems to have recognized him for who he truly is: Cormac Mac Art the riever, except a young warrior named Hakon. Other than McOthna/Mac Art, only one character is not a Norseman in this congregation of sea-wolves: Brulla, a chief of the Picts. Hates and resentment are smoldering, and Cormac's arrival is the spark that sets off the powder keg.

Commentary: Robert E. Howard to Tevis Clyde Smith, circa May 1930:

"I am confronted with the enigma of editors. They say they want action stuff. Well, I have a story with *Argosy* which I am certain they will reject as I am that I'm sitting here. Yet it bristles with fast, well-written action. There is a perfect shimmer of swords from the opening scene where Thorwald Shield-hewer throws a drinking-horn of ale in the face of chief Brulla of Hjaltlands, to the scene on Hakon's Skel's dragon-ship where Cormac Mac Art unmasks the Mysterious Stranger and Wulfhere Hausakliufr roars: 'Aim her prow east, carles, we go to set a new king on the throne of Dane-mark!' By golly, whatever else they may say about that story, they can't kick about the action. I consider it my best attempt of the sort, to date. But will I sell it? Like Hell I will."

Argosy magazine to Howard, 3 June 1930: "Dear Mr. Howard: I'm afraid 'The Night of the Wolf' is a lot too vague and slow moving for *Argosy*."

"The Night of the Wolf" is without a doubt one of Howard's fastest-moving action tales, a riveting page-turner from beginning to end.

Chapter Five
A Few Laconic Words on Ten Other Tales

"The Curse of Greed"

Because one needs to read at least one of Howard's "confession stories." This one is about a bootlegger whose bad whiskey caused his daughter to go blind, which in turn led to his wife committing suicide, not to mention his son dying while he was working for the bootlegger's competitor. All that, and repentance, in nine pages.

"Daughters of Feud"

Because one needs to read at least one of Howard's "spicy" tales, potboilers written in the last months of his life to make some quick and easy money. This is, and by far, the wildest of those.

"A Matter of Age"

Because, upon reflection, one needs to read not one, but two of Howard's confession tales, including this one, written in the first person, supposedly by a fifteen-year old "fine-bodied" girl looking much older than her age… Highly enjoyable if read just like it was written: with a nod and a wink.

"The House"

Because, when Howard writes about the life of poet Justin Geoffrey, surrounded by frighteningly prosaic people, he is writing about himself.

"Wolfshead"

Because mixing so many characters with a plot that stretches the boundaries of verisimilitude way too far, in a setting that is absolutely unbelievable even for a single instant, and managing to pull it out nonetheless, is a true testimony to the budding genius that was Howard's in 1925.

"The Black Moon"

Because detective Steve Harrison manages to arrest his man, having noticed that the buddha was the green one, not the blue (or maybe the other way round), though it turns out that this all-too crucial detail didn't matter after all since the killer was color-blind. A perfect illustration of Howard's difficulties with classic detective stories: "I have definitely abandoned the detective field, where I never had any success anyway, and which represents a type of story I actively detest. I can scarcely endure to read one, much less write one."

"The Pool of the Black One"

Because, whatever one may think of that Conan story, it is absolutely impossible to justify Sancha's nudity in the first chapter.

"Bran Mak Morn: a Play"

Because even if a juvenile effort, writing a play starring Bran Mak Morn required quite some nerve.

"The Cat and the Skull"

Because to change one's mind as to the identity of the foe in the middle of the story and keep on writing the tale without taking the time to rewrite a few pages or even paragraphs, required even more nerve.

"The God in the Bowl"

Because even if the third Conan story isn't one of Howard's best by any stretch, the way Howard portrays the power plays between civilized people and the difference of treatment between the haves and the have-nots by the "authorities" hasn't aged a day. Not even a second.

> *"By the way, did you notice where a coon cooked three cops in New Orleans? All they were doing, according to the papers, was giving him the once over with a rubber hose in his cell, when the ungrateful cur grabbed one of their gats and cooked three of them. Then he fought off several scores of them for hours, until they finally got him. Thk, thk, thk. What's the country coming to when the cops can't beat up an ungrateful coon without risking their lives? Such duplicity is detestable to behold. No doubt some other coon will pay for it—and maybe this time they'll remember to handcuff him. Even a dog is likely to bite you if you kick him often enough."*
>
> *— Robert E. Howard to Tevis Clyde Smith, reacting to events which took place on March 10, 1932. The letter was sent just before Howard wrote "The God in the Bowl."*

"A great poet is greater than any king." – Conan

Chapter Six
The Real Conan . . . and the Imitations

The observation is simple: more people come to Howard via Conan than the other way round. And even more than that: more people come to Howard by way of a Conan that is not Howard's Conan, but that of the movies, the comics, the games, or the pastiches; and many of those—until very recently—shared very few common traits with the original creation. Conan's notoriety has helped sell books and was a definite factor in Howard's popularity, but at what price? Whoever said that any publicity is good should perhaps study what happened with Howard.

1. Is it mandatory to hear the lamentations of their women, late at night, in the vastness of the steppes?

Chief: We won again! This is good, but what is best in life?

Warrior: The open steppe, a fleet horse, falcons at your wrist, and the wind in your hair.

Chief: Wrong! Conan! What is best in life?

Conan: Crush your enemies. See them driven before you. Hear the lamentations of their women.

Chief: That is good! That is good.

– John Milius, *Conan the Barbarian* (1982)

Here is the dialogue most associated to Conan in the public's mind. Ask anyone not familiar with Howard about Conan, and nine times out of ten, this is what they are going mention. Except of course that Howard's Conan never utters those words, or anything remotely close. That is not surprising, given how Milius' grandiloquent and martial philosophy is so exactly the opposite of Howard's prose and leanings. This being said, if the quote owes its popularity to Milius, it doesn't originate with him.

His Conan movie is essentially an homage to Genghis Khan. Milius, a "Zen fascist" (as he describes himself), has always entertained the idea of directing a movie about the Mongol conqueror, and was still thinking about it in 2010 when he had his stroke. It is this fascination for the subject which explains the name Subotai, Conan's friend in the movie: the real Subotai was one of the Khan's most trusted lieutenants. The only link that can be established between the movie and Howard is that Howard had read *Genghis Khan, Emperor of all Men*, the 1924 biography written by Harold Lamb, and so had Milius, understandably so given his interest in the subject. Milius' interest in the subject can be seen in this most interesting exchange taken from Lamb's book:

> One day in the pavilion at Karakorum he asked an officer of the Mongol guard what, in all the world, could bring the greatest happiness.

> "The open steppe, a clear day, and a swift horse under you," responded the officer after a little thought, "and a falcon on your wrist to start up hares."

> "Nay," responded the Khan, "to crush your enemies, to see them fall at your feet—to take their horses and goods and hear the lamentation of their women. That is best."

Genghis the Barbarian? Probably. An excellent movie and an unforgettable score? Yes, indeed. A movie that has anything to do with Howard's Conan? Absolutely not.

2. Conan leaves his homeland because he wants to become a king.

This notion is not found anywhere in Howard, contrary to popular belief. It is somewhat present in the Milius movie, but it is mostly due to L. Sprague de Camp that we owe this modification of the Cimmerian's life, changed from an ode to freedom into a career plan.

By creating the myth of the slow ascension of a barbarian up the rungs of the social ladder (thief, warrior, mercenary, general, king), de

Camp gave the readers the illusion of a logical progression in the "career" of the Cimmerian. Again, this is not to be found anywhere in Howard. The Texan did write three tales portraying Conan as king of Aquilonia (in two of which, incidentally, he has lost his throne to usurpers.) But his accession to kingship was not the result of a carefully laid out plan: the opportunity presented itself one day, and Conan seized it, not because it corresponded to the achievement of a lifelong ambition, but because it is in Conan's nature to seize a good opportunity when he sees one, if he feels like it. de Camp knew this and had to "fix" a section of "The Black Stranger" to make the story fit *his* conception of the series, as well as write tales of his own that would fill what he perceived as "holes in the saga."

In "Beyond the Black River," Conan says this:

> "I've been a mercenary captain, a corsair, a kozak, a penniless vagabond, a general—hell, I've been everything except a king, and I may be that, before I die." The fancy pleased him, and he grinned hardly. Then he shrugged his shoulders and stretched his mighty figure on the rocks. "This is as good a life as any. I don't know how long I'll stay on the frontier; a week, a month, a year. I have a roving foot. But it's as well on the border as anywhere."

And in "Red Nails":

> "I've never been king of an Hyborian kingdom," he grinned, taking an enormous mouthful of cactus. "But I've dreamed of being even that. I may be too, some day. Why shouldn't I?"

De Camp's obsession for the slow ascension from lowly—despicable—origins (thief) to the heights of—respectable—society, conforms to the typical conception of the American "success story," a none-too-subtle Hyborian variation on the rags-to-riches story: a young man coming from a foreign country, starting out with nothing but a wish to succeed, who eventually reaches the pinnacle of success. (One can readily see how Arnold Schwarzenegger could easily identify with the character that made him famous.) Whoever reads the three stories showing Conan as king of Aquilonia soon understands that Howard's conception of kingship couldn't be further away from the destiny of an ambitious adventurer imposing his iron will on a subjugated people. In Howard, the king is first and foremost at the service of his people, and is more often than not crushed by the duties of the royal function. Turlogh O'Brien and Bran Mak Morn, two other Howard characters who become kings, are identical examples.

3. Cimmeria.

Cimmeria is the country of Conan's origins, and it is also because of Cimmeria that Conan is who he is. When we read the Conan tales, we encounter numerous Turanians, Aquilonians or Bossonians. However, there is no Cimmerian character other than Conan. One only has to read the first version of the first tale in the series, "The Phoenix on the Sword," (this draft published in *The Coming of Conan the Cimmerian*, Del Rey Books, 2003) to understand the exact nature of that land: it is a terrible region, gloomy, and the mere act of thinking about it leads Conan to drink alcohol to seek oblivion. As described in the poem of the same name, the country is dull, dark, and menacing. We can thus say that Conan has left Cimmeria as much because he wanted to flee it as he wanted to roam the world. Perhaps more than because he wanted to roam the world…

4. Who was the real inspiration behind Conan?

There are quite a number of answers to this question, but no single satisfying one. From a strictly literary viewpoint, the first Conan tale was but the rewrite of an unsold Kull of Atlantis tale written in 1929. One could thus argue that Conan and Kull are identical. They are only alike physically, however (though Kull is grey-eyed and Conan blue-eyed). Conan is a Cimmerian, which, in Howard's conception of the Hyborian world, makes him a protohistorical Irish Gael. In that respect, the other Howard character he is closest to is not Kull, but the savage and grim Cormac Fitzgeoffrey (Irish origins, blue eyes, swears by Crom).

Howard once explained that:

Conan simply grew up in my mind a few years ago when I was stopping in a little border town on the lower Rio Grande. I did not create him by any conscious process. He simply stalked full grown out of oblivion and set me at work recording the saga of his adventures.

He added that:

> He is simply a combination of a number of men I have known, and I think that's why he seemed to step full-grown into my consciousness when I wrote the first yarn of the series. Some mechanism in my subconsciousness took the dominant characteristics of various prizefighters, gunmen, bootleggers, oil field bullies, gamblers, and honest workmen I had come in contact with, and combining them all, produced the amalgamation I call Conan the Cimmerian.

One should not take Howard at face value here, as is often the case for such statements. When he created the character, in 1932, he was just starting to develop an interest in the history of the Southwest and the gunfighters, but not sufficiently to influence him so importantly on the Conan stories. Conan may thus be a "combination," as Howard writes, but the sources behind his most famous creations are varied and diverse.

Arnold Schwarzenegger (left) as Conan; Jason Momoa (right) as Conan.

5. Arnold or Jason?

Howard systematically describes Conan as a powerful man, but also as very supple, able to climb a cliff using only his hands. When it comes to metaphors, the Cimmerian is usually compared to a great cat or panther, who can move at an impressive speed. Howard also tells us that Conan speaks many languages, that "he had squatted for hours in the courtyards of the philosophers, listening to the arguments of theologians and teachers," and one only needs read the stories to quickly realize that Conan can speak quite eloquently when he wants to.

When all this is factored in, is it really necessary to add that Conan never punches any camel in the stories?

It took Farnsworth Wright many months before he realized the commercial potential of Conan. The first three stories ("The Phoenix on the Sword," "The Scarlet Citadel" and "Tower of the Elephant") were published without being cover-featured or even mentioned on the cover. The fourth was "Black Colossus" (June 1933 issue). The cover, painted by Margaret Brundage depicts a nude Yasmela imploring the statue of her god, but the Cimmerian is nowhere to be seen. The next Conan story was "Xuthal of the Dusk." Brundage's cover shows a scantily-clad Thalis whipping an equally nude Natala. Here again the Cimmerian is nowhere to be seen. It's only when "Queen of the Black Coast" was published (May 1934) that Conan made his first appearance on the cover. He was present a second time in August ("The Devil in Iron") and a third in 1935 (The Hour of the Dragon). All the other covers feature scantily-clad women and no Conan. As to "Beyond the Black River", one of the best tales in the series, published as a serial, it wasn't even cover-featured. There are no female characters of note in that story, and this very probably explains that.

6. Conan and Women.

The public is usually unable to imagine Conan without a whimpering woman clinging to him in a state of undress that the weather can't even begin to justify, and whose tendency to open the wrong door or be captured by a more or less octopoid monster seems to defy the odds. Was the Texan responsible, or even guilty, of this sorry state of affairs?

The answer is yes... and no. Yes, because in the second half of 1932, Howard suddenly found himself short of several regular markets, victims of the Depression. His only regular market was *Weird Tales*, which published the Conan stories. The magazine had just hired a new cover artist, Margaret Brundage, who excelled at depicting nude or semi-nude women. Howard, in dire need of money, took notice, and slanted his next stories so that they included a scene that could potentially be selected for a cover illustration. When Howard's financial situation took a turn for the better a few months later, he began writing Conan tales featuring more rounded out female characters, culminating with Valeria of the Red Brotherhood in "Red Nails."

The first Conan stories (composed between March and September 1932) do not feature a single damsel in distress, the only two female characters of note being Atali (a goddess) and Bêlit (the queen of the Black Coast). Beginning with "People of the Black Circle" (January 1934), Howard's heroines are for the most part quite temperamental and interesting: Yasmina (Devi of Vendhya), Gitara (a spy and a schemer, who has her lover Khemsa under her thumb), Zelata (an aged witch), Zenobia (a slave who risks her life to save Conan), Belesa and Tina (a young woman and a child), and Valeria the she-pirate (who scoffs at Conan's advances). Granted, they are not all exempt from stereotyping, but they are far, very far, from the kind of women usually associated with the Cimmerian.

Most pastichers—De Camp, Lin Carter and others—as well as the Marvel Comics version of Conan have much more contributed to the image of a macho-Conan than the few weaker tales written by Howard. Not one admirer of Howard would ever rank those stories in his or her best-of list.

Title	Date Written	Dependant Female Character	Strong Female Character
"The Phoenix on the Sword"	Feb-32		
"The Frost Giant's Daughter"	Feb-32		X
"The God in the Bowl"	Mar-32		
"The Tower of the Elephant"	Mar-32		
"The Scarlet Citadel"	Apr-32		
"Queen of the Black Coast"	Jul-32		X
Fight Stories, *Action Stories*, and *Strange Tales* go out of business.			
"Black Colossus"	Sep-32	X	
"Iron Shadows in the Moon"	Oct-32	X	
"Xuthal of the Dusk"	Nov-32	X	X
"The Pool of the Black One"	Nov-32	X	
"Rogues in the House"	Dec-32		
"Vale of the Lost Women"	Feb-33	X	
Howard hires an agent. Sales begin to soar again beginning in June 1933			
"The Devil in Iron"	Oct-33	X	
"People of the Black Circle"	Jan-34		X
The Hour of the Dragon	Mar-34		X
"A Witch Shall be Born"	Jun-34		X
"The Servants of Bit-Yakin"	Jul-34	X	
"Beyond the Black River"	Aug-34		
"The Black Stranger"	late 1934		X
"The Man-Eaters of Zamboula"	early 1935		X
"Red Nails"	Jul-35		X

7. Bêlit, Valeria or Red Sonja? Does Conan have a regular girl-friend?

Red Sonja is not a Howard creation. Bêlit is not Conan's great love (he doesn't cry after she dies: Marvel Comics' Conan does). As for Valeria, she scoffs at the Cimmerian's attempts at seducing her. Granted, she is less fiery at the end of the story, but her physical and mental exhaustion after what happened in Xuchotl explain that. Conan has no more relationships in his biography than James Bond.

With every new story, the reader encounters new situations and new characters, male and female. Only Conan remains the same, being a given.

8. Conan... the Barbarian?

Sherlock Holmes never utters the words he is most famous for—"Elementary, my dear Watson"—in any of the 60 tales Sir Arthur Conan Doyle devoted to his character. By the same token, it should come as no surprise that Howard never uses the expression "Conan the Barbarian" anywhere. "Conan the Barbarian" is a pop-culture icon, a pastiche character, a movie character. Howard wrote tales featuring a Cimmerian named Conan.

9. The true Conan in quotes.

"The carven door closed behind the Poitanian, and Conan turned back to his task. And suddenly the mask of his mirth fell away from him like a mask. His face was suddenly old, his eyes worn. The unreasoning melancholy of the Cimmerian fell like a shroud about his soul, paralyzing him with a sense of crushing futility. His kingship, his ambitions and all earthly things seemed as dust. The borders of life shrivelled and the lines closed in about him, crushing him. Dropping his lion head in his mighty hands, he groaned aloud.

"Then lifting his head, as a man looks for escape, his eyes fell on a crystal jar of yellow wine. Quickly he rose and pouring a goblet full, quaffed it at a gulp. Again he filled and emptied the goblet, and again. This time when he set it down, a fine warmth stole through his veins. Facts and events assumed new values. The grey Cimmerian hills faded far behind him."

–"The Phoenix on the Sword", first version

"'What do I know of cultured ways, the gilt, the craft and the lie?
'I, who was born in a naked land and bred in the open sky.
'The subtle tongue, the sophist guile, they fail when the broadswords sing'
'Rush in and die, dogs—I was a man before I was a king.'"

—"The Phoenix on the Sword")

Civilized men are more discourteous than savages because they know they can be impolite without having their skulls split, as a general thing.

—"The Tower of the Elephant"

"I have known many gods. He who denies them is as blind as he who trusts them too deeply. I seek not beyond death. It may be the blackness averred by the Nemedian skeptics, or Crom's realm of ice and cloud, or the snowy plains and vaulted halls of the Nordheimer's Valhalla. I know not, nor do I care. Let me live deep while I live; let me know the rich juices of red meat and stinging wine on my palate, the hot embrace of white arms, the mad exultation of battle when the blue blades flame and crimson, and I am content. Let teachers and priests and philosophers brood over questions of reality and illusion. I know this: if life is illusion, then I am no less an illusion, and being thus, the illusion is real to me. I live, I burn with life, I love, I slay, and am content."

—"Queen of the Black Coast"

"What are you but an adventurer, seizing a crown to which you had no more claim than any other wandering barbarian?" parried Amalrus. "We are prepared to offer you suitable compensation—"

"Compensation!" it was a gust of deep laughter from Conan's mighty chest. "The price of infamy and treachery! I am a barbarian, so I shall sell my kingdom and its people for life and your filthy gold? Ha! How did you come to your crown, you and that black-faced pig beside you? Your fathers did the fighting and the suffering, and handed their crowns to you on golden platters. What you inherited without lifting a finger—except to poison a few brothers—I fought for.

"You sit on satin and guzzle wine the people sweat for, and talk of divine rights of sovereignty—bah! I climbed out of the abyss of naked barbarism to the throne and in that climb I spilt my blood as freely as I spilt that of others. If either of us has the right to rule men, by Crom, it is I! How have you proved yourself my superior?

"I found Aquilonia in the grip of a pig like you—one who traced his genealogy for a thousand years. The land was torn with the wars of the barons, and the people cried out under oppression and taxation. Today no Aquilonian noble dares maltreat the humblest of my subjects, and the taxes of the people are lighter than anywhere else in the world.

"What of you? Your brother, Amalrus, holds the eastern half of your kingdom and defies you. And you, Strabonus, your soldiers are even now besieging castles of a dozen or more rebellious barons. The people of both your kingdoms are crushed into the earth by tyrannous taxes and levies. And you would loot mine—ha! Free my hands and I'll varnish this floor with your brains!"

—"The Scarlet Citadel"

The woodsman sighed and stared at his calloused hand, worn from contact with ax-haft and sword-hilt. Conan reached his long arm for the wine-jug. The forester stared at him, comparing him with the men about them, the men who had died along the lost river, comparing him with those other wild men over that river. Conan did not seem aware of his gaze.

"Barbarism is the natural state of mankind," the borderer said, still staring somberly at the Cimmerian. "Civilization is unnatural. It is a whim of circumstance. And barbarism must always ultimately triumph."

—"Beyond the Black River"

"There's nothing in the universe cold steel won't cut."

—"Beyond the Black River"

"Let others dream imperial dreams. I but wish to hold what is mine. I have no desire to rule an empire welded together by blood and fire. It's one thing to seize a throne with the aid of its subjects and rule them with their consent. It's another to subjugate a foreign realm and rule it by fear. I don't wish to be another Valerius. No, Trocero, I'll rule all Aquilonia and no more, or I'll rule nothing."

—*The Hour of the Dragon*

"Well, last night in a tavern, a captain in the king's guard offered violence to the sweetheart of a young soldier, who naturally ran him through. But it seems there is some cursed law against killing guardsmen, and the boy and his girl fled away. It was bruited about that I was seen with them, and so today I was haled into court, and a judge asked me where the lad had gone. I replied that since he was a friend of mine, I could not betray him. Then the court waxed wroth, and the judge talked a great deal about my duty to the state, and society, and other things I did not understand, and bade me tell where my friend had flown. By this time I was becoming wrathful myself, for I had explained my position.

"But I choked my ire and held my peace, and the judge squalled that I had shown contempt for the court, and that I should be hurled into a dungeon to rot until I betrayed my friend. So then, seeing they were all mad, I drew my sword and cleft the judge's skull; then I cut my way out of the court, and seeing the high constable's stallion tied near by, I rode for the wharfs, where I thought to find a ship bound for foreign parts."

–"Queen of the Black Coast"

"Who are you?" she asked. "Shah Amurath called you a *kozak;* were you of that band?"

"I am Conan, of Cimmeria," he grunted. "I was with the *kozaki,* as the Hyrkanian dogs called us."

She knew vaguely that the land he named lay far to the northwest, beyond the farthest boundaries of the different kingdoms of her race.

"I am a daughter of the king of Ophir," she said. "My father sold me to a Shemite chief, because I would not marry a prince of Koth."

The Cimmerian grunted in surprize.

Her lips twisted in a bitter smile. "Aye, civilized men sell their children as slaves to savages, sometimes. They call your race barbaric, Conan of Cimmeria."

"We do not sell our children," he growled, his chin jutting truculently.

–"Iron Shadows in the Moon"

"The best land near Thunder River is already taken," grunted the slayer. "Plenty of good land between Scalp Creek—you crossed it a few miles back—and the fort, but that's getting too devilish close to the river. The Picts steal over to burn and murder—as that one did. They don't always come singly. Some day they'll try to sweep the settlers out of Conajohara. And they may succeed—probably will succeed. This colonization business is mad, anyway. There's plenty of good land east of the Bossonian marches. If the Aquilonians would cut up some of the big estates of their barons, and plant wheat where now only deer are hunted, they wouldn't have to cross the border and take the land of the Picts away from them."

"That's queer talk from a man in the service of the Governor of Conajohara," objected Balthus.

"It's nothing to me," the other retorted. "I'm a mercenary. I sell my sword to the highest bidder. I never planted wheat and never will, so long as there are other harvests to be reaped with the sword.

—"Beyond the Black River"

"Conan, the Cimmerian!" ejaculated the woman. "What are *you* doing on my trail?"

He grinned hardly, and his fierce blue eyes burned with a light any woman could understand as they ran over her magnificent figure, lingering on the swell of her splendid breasts beneath the light shirt, and the clear white flesh displayed between breeches and boot-tops.

"Don't you know?" he laughed. "Haven't I made my admiration for you plain ever since I first saw you?"

"A stallion could have made it no plainer," she answered disdainfully.

—"Red Nails"

10. Canonic Conan

At the end of the 1990s, British publisher Wandering Star acquired the rights to the Conan stories, which had been in its sights since day one. The first worldwide edition of the Conan tales as written by Robert E. Howard without any editorial tampering was about to hit the market.

Wandering Star was, first and foremost, a film production company, which had bought the movie rights to Solomon. It was Marcelo Anciano, art director of the project and its true mastermind, who decided to spend the promotional budget in an original way. In order to seduce Hollywood people (agents, actors and directors), Anciano imagined and conceived a sumptuous illustrated book in the tradition of the deluxe volumes of the late nineteenth and early twentieth century, where the non-literary aspects of the book (binding, gilding, illustration, design) were deemed as important as the actual contents. Anciano's reasoning was that movie people would be convinced with their eyes, not their brains, and thus they needed a visual stimulant: a beautiful edition and top-notch illustrations. He wanted to present Howard as a "classic" author, on a par with Jack London or Robert Louis Stevenson. Perfectly aware of the editorial tribulations of the Howard stories, he enlisted the aid of Rusty Burke, the leading Howard scholar, as series editor. Published in 1998 to rave reviews, *The Savage Tales of Solomon Kane* didn't immediately lead to the expected movie, which wouldn't become a reality for another fifteen years. But Anciano remained on board with what he called the "Howard Library" and next published *Bran Mak Morn: The Last King* and *The Ultimate Triumph* (the latter being Howard tales illustrated by Frank Frazetta).

When the Conan deal was signed, the expectations from the fans were extremely high, as was the the volume of work required. It was then common knowledge among the fans that many of the stories in earlier editions had been tampered with, rewritten and/or completed by the previous editors. What these pure Howard texts look like? Who would be the new illustrator whose task would be to make the readers forget Frazetta? How many volumes, what order for the stories, and what sources for the texts?

Anciano opted to have a different illustrator for each Conan volume. The Conan tales were sufficiently rich to allow for varied interpretations. Then he and Burke asked this author if he wanted to edit the books.

Three years before, my first serious attempt at Howard scholarship had been published in *The Dark Man, the Journal of Robert E. Howard Studies*, edited by the same Rusty Burke. Titled "The Birth of Conan" in a tongue-in-cheek way, my aim was to explain how Conan was really born: not on a battlefield, but in February 1932 on a typewritten sheet of paper. The essay established a timeline showing the order in which Howard wrote the Conan stories, a task that had been considered as impossible by many. It was this essay (and a knowledge of what I was working on), that convinced Burke to suggest Anciano to hire this Frenchman as editor of the Conan volumes.

At that time, the project was still vague in its conception, but two things were clear in my mind: the stories should be published in the order they were written, with the exception of the unfinished tales and fragments, which should be relegated to the appendices, and not be part of the main body of the book (since Howard himself had opted not to complete them). Conversely, the stories not published in *Weird Tales* were reintegrated in the main body. Wright's tastes and decisions didn't matter seventy years after the fact. The new presentation—stories appearing in the order of writing and all the fragments left in their unedited state in the back section of the book—broke with thirty-five years of the editorial practice which gave the so-called biography of Conan precedence over the evolution and maturing of Howard as an author. The planned four-volume edition was brought back to three, (just like that other monument of modern fantasy). Last, I wanted the books to conclude with a series of dense critical essays, who would to put to rest the stupidities that had plagued Howard and Conan criticism for decades, and offer the readers fresh insight and background on the stories.

Thanks to my friendship with Glenn Lord, former agent for the Howard heirs, I had been slowly accumulating thousands of copies of original Howard typescripts and had spent a good amount of time developing techniques to date these, based on various elements (idiosyncrasies, presentation, spelling mistakes, typewriter quirks, etc.) as part of my personal researches. When I was officially appointed editor of the series, this task was already well under way and close to completion (though "The Vale of Lost Women" resisted my efforts for many weeks). If Glenn owned the immense majorities of the surviving Howard papers, I knew a few Conan typescripts were in private hands, and I had been tracking them down. I eventually obtained copies of each of those, with two exceptions: a draft for "A Witch shall be Born" (where I received a flat "no") and, maybe, the final version for "Queen of the Black Coast," supposedly extant and out there, and which has been buried in a collection (or maybe two) since 1984.

Weird Tales, just like most pulp magazines, trashed the typescripts

The author (right) with Glenn Lord (left) in 2009.

once the story had been typeset, and thus many of the final versions of Howard's tales are lost forever, with a few exceptions. Fortunately, Howard kept everything, and in his archives were many carbon copies of the final version. Also, he had been sent back a few typescripts, probably in answer to the request of a few collectors. Robert H. Barlow, Lovecraft's young protégé, was an avid Howard and Conan fan, who eventually had 6, or maybe 7, Conan typescripts in his collection. The comparison between the carbons and the versions as published in *Weird Tales* revealed that the editor of the magazine censored what few lines of dialogues he deemed too "spicy" or profane. Tiberias the merchant, in "Beyond the Black River," a "fat bastard" in Howard's typescript thus became a "fat fool" in the published version. The Wandering Star edition's policy being absolute respect to Howard's text and to correct only what few spelling mistakes or typos there were, all the stories were published from Howard's final version or carbon, and from the *Weird Tales* text if no better source survives.

The three volumes quickly became the standard—authoritative—edition of the Conan tales, and were used as the basis for the trade paperback edition issued by Del Rey Books starting in 2003. Foreign editions are now systematically based on those three volumes.

Now in the position to separate the wheat from the chaff, readers and scholars could at last see what Conan—Howard's Conan—was really all about. A few years down the road, the impact is evident: Modiphius' Conan role-playing game and Monolith's wildly successful Conan tabletop board game use only the Howard tales as their sources, having hired Howard experts to ensure that they would remain true to the source material. At the other end of the spectrum, one can see a definite interest in Howard from the academic field, worldwide. The first step before any form of academic recognition being the ready availability of a standard, uniform and recognized edition had taken decades, not years, delaying serious critical study of Howard by that many years.

"I'll say one thing about an oil boom: it will teach a kid that Life's a pretty rotten thing about as quick as anything I can think of."

– Robert E. Howard

Chapter Seven
About Howard

1. Howard and Lovecraft, Best Enemies?

The correspondence between Robert E. Howard and H.P. Lovecraft is without a doubt one of the most important and fascinating in the domain of imaginative fiction. Lovecraft requires no introduction, hailed as the first star contributor to *Weird Tales* when the magazine was still in its infancy. Howard discovered Lovecraft very early. An unsent (or unpublished) letter by Howard recently surfaced, probably dating from 1926, in which he lauds the talent of HPL. Another letter sent to *Weird Tales* is equally emphatic: "Mr. Lovecraft's latest story, 'The Call of Cthulhu,' is indeed a masterpiece, which I am sure will live as one of the highest achievements of literature. Mr. Lovecraft holds a unique position in the literary world; he has grasped, to all intents, the worlds outside our paltry ken. His scope is unlimited and his range is cosmic. He has the rare gift of making the unreal seem very real and terrible, without lessening the sensation of horror attendant thereto. He touches peaks in his tales which no modern or ancient writer has ever hinted. Sentences and phrases leap suddenly at the reader, as if in utter blackness of solar darkness a door were suddenly flung open, whence flamed the red fire of Purgatory and through which might be momentarily glimpsed monstrous and nightmarish shapes. Herbert Spencer may have been right when he said that it was beyond the human mind to grasp the Unknowable, but Mr. Lovecraft is in a fair way of disproving that theory, I think. I await his next story with eager anticipation, knowing that whatever the subject may be, it will be handled with the skill and incredible vision which he has always shown." Lovecraft had also taken notice of the efforts of the young Howard: "I first became conscious of him as a coming leader just a decade ago—when (on a bench in Prospect Park, Brooklyn) I read "Wolfshead." I had read his two previous short tales with pleasure, but without especially noting the author. Now—in '26—I saw that W.T. had landed a new big-timer

H. P. Lovecraft

of the CAS and EHP calibre. Nor was I ever disappointed in the zestful and vigorous newcomer. He made good—and how!"

The two men wouldn't start corresponding until 1930, though, when Howard took the excuse of a reprint of HPL's "The Rats in the Wall" to send a letter to Farnsworth Wright, inquiring as to HPL's odd use of the Gaelic rather Brythonic dialect at the end of the story, thinking that perhaps Lovecraft shared his unorthodox views on the settlement of the British Isles. Wright's notions on the question were probably every bit as foggy as anyone, and he merely forwarded the letter to Lovecraft. Actually, the latter had simply lifted the passage in question from a story by Fiona McLeod, thinking no one would notice. Wrongly, it turned out. He quickly sent a letter to Howard, thus initiating what would become a voluminous correspondence that would only end when Howard died.

First limited to Celtic linguistics and civilization, the scope of their exchanges soon broadened to include a wide array of subjects. Howard was visibly impressed, even awed, by his Providence colleague, and in a matter of weeks, his literary efforts aimed at *Weird Tales* took a Lovecraftian turn. The volume of Howard's letters to his Texas friends dwindled rapidly, while those exchanged with Lovecraft and, soon enough, members of the "Lovecraft circle" grew in size as well as numbers. It took a few months for Howard to realize he had been aping Lovecraft, producing tales that were, for the most part, unsatisfying and quite unlike him. His later efforts do show some Lovecraft influence at times, but by this time Howard was intentionally playing with his friend's work, who encouraged the practice; hence, the reference to Cthulhu in the first Conan tale, or the few lovecraftian monsters one encounters in some tales.

149

While always very polite toward each other at the beginning, it soon became clear that the two men were diametrically opposed on about everything. After a while, Howard became much more virulent when confronted with Lovecraft's often condescending tone and started replying in a vehement tone. While they sincerely admired the works of the other (though Lovecraft lamented that Howard was not really writing weird fiction anymore), many of the tales Howard wrote for *Weird Tales* during those years were fueled by their exchanges. We have already mentioned "Pigeons from Hell" as an obvious answer to Lovecraft's conception of horror. In the same vein, the unfinished novel *Almuric* (early 1934) can be read as a indirect, literary, refutation of Lovecraft's arguments during their year-long debate on "mental vs. physical" (with professor Hildebrandt as the all-too-rare scientific caution as to the importance of the physical). "Wild Water" also owes something to their exchanges on "Eastern" (i.e. East of the Mississippi) scientists and their limited understanding of the Southwest.

The letters they exchanged in the last two years of Howard's life contain some very bitter paragraphs, as well as scathing attacks by a Howard who had the utmost difficulties dealing with Lovecraft's often peremptory affirmations.

In 1936, Lovecraft was devastated by the news of Howard's death, and it took a number of weeks before he could deal with the loss of this correspondent of six years, a man he had never met. His eulogy, "In Memoriam," published a few months later, remains one of the most perceptive analyses of Howard ever.

2. The Pulp Magazines

Thanks to Quentin Tarantino, everyone has heard of the pulps, but most people have no real idea as to what they were. When Howard began writing professionally in 1921 (aged 15), they were taking their definitive form: squarebound magazines of 128 to 196 pages, printed on the cheapest paper available (wood pulp, hence their name), with bright covers (that would soon become particularly lurid), featuring a number of tales, usually (but not always) a serial or two (to ensure the reader would buy the next issue). The most prestigious were *Adventure*, *Blue Book* and *Argosy*, sporting better paper and a higher literary quality. These few respectable publications competed

Weird Tales *was the premier fantasy and horror pulp of the 1920s and 1930s.*

against hundreds of titles, many of which lasted only a few issues, cheap imitations of their prestigious cousins, often with a narrower subject matter: *Thrilling Adventures, Zeppelin Stories, Jack Dempsey's Fight Magazine,* etc.

Many of the publishing houses were fly-by-night operations, artwork could be recycled from one magazine to another, and sometimes the stories themselves, often without the author's knowledge. Outré situations and titillation were definitely more important than literary quality. The pulps offered the average American cheap entertainment at a time when America was plunged into the Great Depression. Their decline began in 1938, shortly after the appearance of Superman and the explosion of super-heroes. Sold for about the same price, incredibly cheap to produce, the comics were way more lucrative and drove the pulps out of the newsstands.

3. *Weird Tales*

Weird Tales appeared on the newsstands in March 1923, the brainchild of one William Sprenger, who wanted to publish a magazine entirely devoted to the weird. (A previous effort—*The Thrill Book*—

the contents of which included some fantastic tales, had failed to meet with success in 1919 though it did apparently have very limited circulation).

Edwin Baird, *Weird Tales'* first editor, tried many formats for the magazine, to no avail. The real problem was in the contents. There is simply nothing worth saving from the pulp's first year of publication. The stories were, for the most, simply abysmal or undistinguished, forgotten as soon as they are read. The only exceptions were the first tales of H.P. Lovecraft who was making his professional debut in the new magazine. Tens of thousands of dollars in debt, the future of *Weird Tales* was far from bright. Lovecraft was offered Baird's position, but he turned it down: he would have had to relocate to Chicago (where the *Weird Tales* offices were) and he had just married Sonia Greene. Since it was highly probable that the magazine would not survive very long, his refusal is easily understandable. It was Farnsworth Wright, another writer, who took the job. He would prove to be a much better editor than author, if the few tales published in the magazine are any indication. His first task was to publish all the inventory stories, to start hunting for new talent and to encourage those he felt had real potential, like Clark Ashton Smith (who only had a few poems published in *Weird Tales* by that time), Henry S. Whitehead, or Seabury Quinn (whose early tales did show potential). His first new discovery, who would soon become his protégé, was a young Robert E. Howard. The two men developed a particular working relationship, fruitful if strained at times, for the next ten years. Wright never ceased giving Howard advice and encouraging him. He did reject many a tale, but in the immense majority of the cases, those rejections were justified, or at least well-intentioned. Wright would prove much less visionary when it came to Lovecraft.

Weird Tales is remembered today because of the talents who published their most famous works in its pages, most notably Howard, Lovecraft and Smith, but also Catherine Moore, Manly Wade Wellman and others, but at the time, the most popular writer of the magazine was Seabury Quinn and his tales of Jules de Grandin, now all but forgotten. In 1939, afflicted with Parkinson's disease, his best authors either dead, retired, or alienated (due to the pulp's chronic financial difficulties), Wright was replaced by Dorothy McIlwraith, effectively putting an end to the magazine's golden age. Of tremendous literary quality when compared to most contemporary pulps' standards, graced with superb covers by Margaret Brundage, Virgil Finlay and John Allen St. John, *Weird Tales* was truly, for a few years, the 'unique magazine' it boastfully claimed to be on its masthead, in the small world of the pulps.

4. Howard, literary heir to William Morris and Lord Dunsany, or cousin to Dashiell Hammett?

For many years, L. Sprague de Camp and Lin Carter insisted on trying to establish Howard as a worthy (or maybe not-so-worthy) literary heir to the Victorian "medieval romances" of William Morris and to the works of Lord Dunsany. There is nothing, however, in Howard's writings that shows any noticeable degree of influence from these writers, whom he barely mentions in his correspondence. Of Dunsany, he said he had read some of his poetry, and there is no reference to Morris at all. It wasn't until 1984 and the publication of George Knight's seminal "Robert E. Howard: Hard-Boiled Heroic-Fantasist" that the notion of a Howard influenced by these two writers was put to rest. Knight—a pseudonym of Don Herron—argued, in what is one of the most important essays on Howard ever written, that Howard's style and preoccupations couldn't be further away, and established a parallel between what Howard was doing with fantasy to what Dashiell Hammett had been doing to the detective story. If "Hammett took murder out of the Venetian vase and dropped it into the alley," as Raymond Chandler once famously wrote, Knight shows conclusively that Howard was giving an American form to what was until then a purely European genre, getting rid in the process of the Victorian writers' ornate language, refined aesthetics, and their obsession with aristocracy. The Howardian hero is a commoner who has no patience with hereditary monarchy and privileges. The world he lives in offers no hope here or hereafter. It is a constant battlefield in a necessarily corrupt society, fated to extinction, and in which the protagonist can at best hope to survive and forget death for a while. One can readily understand why Howard stated that Conan was a realistic character. There are many more common points between the works of Howard and Hammett—though the two men were writing in different genres and had almost nothing in common—than with the medieval romances and fantasies of the Old Continent writers.

5. Author and Poet

The epitaph "Author and Poet" we can read on Howard's tomb-
stone. He had probably discovered poetry through his mother, herself a lover of literature in general and poetry in particular. This love
of poetry is a trait shared by the three great writers of *Weird Tales*—
Lovecraft, Howard and Smith. Exactly when Howard began writing
verse is not known, but we know that the immense majority of his
poems were composed between 1926 and 1930 (aged 20 to 24). As
every young (and idealistic) writer, he did try several times to have his
verse published, but the collections he submitted were rejected. His
name appears in a series of vanity press publications as well as several
amateur publications, the scarcity of which on the collectors' market
being a reflection of their minuscule print run and obscurity. The only magazine which published his poems with any degree of regularity,
payment and visibility was, once again, *Weird Tales*. But it was impossible to earn a living by writing poetry. Howard explained that he
loved verse, but had to concentrate on paying markets. His production dwindled rapidly after 1930, and he quit writing poems a few
months later, with the occasional exception (notably chapter head-
ings, of which he was excessively fond). It is an impossible task to
properly evaluate the number of poems he wrote, as many of these
were lost or destroyed over the years. A conservative estimate will put
the number at well above a thousand, of which more than seven
hundred have come to us. Howard's verse is firmly rooted in the tradition of the classical poets of the Victorian era, far from the then-
recent modernist revolution. Howard concluded: "My rhyming isn't
of sufficient importance for me to take it seriously, or to bind myself
to any school or rule. I'm no poet but I was born with a knack of
making little words rattle together and I've gotten a bit of pleasure
from my jinglings. I'm willing to let the real poets grind out their images with blood and sweat, and to go through life piping lustily on my
half-penny whistle. Poetizing's work and travail; rhyming's pleasure
and holiday. I never devoted over thirty minutes to any rhyme in my
life, though I've spent hours memorizing the poetry of other men." If
Howard probably devoted little time to most of his poems, quickly
jotted down as spur-of-the-moment ideas, it is obvious that some
required much more effort. He was *Weird Tales'* best versifier with
Clark Ashton Smith. Several volumes of poetry began appearing as

early as 1957, and a particularly thick *Collected Poetry* volume was recently published by the Robert E. Howard Foundation.

6. Collecting Howard

Collecting Howard is a rather fun, though relatively onerous hobby.

The immense majority of Howard's stories were published in pulp magazines. Printed on the cheapest—acidic—paper, those magazines age badly if not stored in proper conditions. Contrary to popular belief, the issues that are the most in demand are not the more difficult to find, nor the more expensive. *Weird Tales* was indeed a niche publication, but many of its readers were fans, the geeks of the 1930s, who were very particular as to condition and took special care of their collection. With a few exceptions, most issues of *Weird Tales* from 1928 onward are easily found. Earlier issues are scarcer, but the very first Howard tale in *Weird Tales*, or even the first Conan (December 1932) will cost the collector five hundred to a thousand time less than the first appearance of Superman (June 1938). The hardest Howard pulps to locate and acquire are the generic titles—*Action Stories, Fight Stories, Sport-Story Magazine*, etc.—pulps that were thrown away as soon as they were read. They are so rare that there is simply no time for second thought: if you find a copy, you buy it, whatever the condition, with the hope of upgrading in the (hopefully not too) distant future.

Fanzines from the 1930s are for the most part relatively easy to find (with the exception of the obscure poetry chapbooks). Here again, there are exceptions, such as the March 1934 issue of *The Fantasy Fan*, in high demand because it features the first appearance of "Gods of the North" a.k.a. "The Frost King's Daughter," a rejected Conan tale, who becomes, in this version, Amra of Akbitana. Other rarities include the issues of *The Phantagraph* serializing "The Hyborian Age" and the 1938 chapbook of the same title, printing the essay in full.

The first landmark Howard book was *Skull-Face and Others*, published by Arkham House in 1946, a compendium of many of his best tales. Printed in an edition of 3,004 copies, the book is easy to find, and only requires deep pockets (usually $300 to $1,000 depending on the condition). This would be followed in 1957 by *Always Comes Evening* (thought at the time to be the complete poetry), in an edition of 636 copies. The dustjacket is often smudged, the black of the front cover having bled on the white of the back cover at print time. Expect to pay a significant premium for a truly Fine copy. The first Conan volume was issued in 1950 by Gnome Press, but it is fairly common. Much scarcer is its British reprint (TV Boardman, 1953), which is simply very rarely found. As a matter of fact, books published in the UK prove to be—and by far—the scarcest Howard collectibles. Before that, Howard had three stories published in three separate volumes of the British anthology series "Not at Night," including the first publication of a Conan tale ("Rogues in the House") in hardcover (*Terror by Night*, 1934). Very fragile, the books of this series are rarely found, and are extremely scarce in dustjacket and/or Fine condition.

The scarcest collectible of all, and the Holy Grail of any serious collector, is the 1937 edition of *A Gent from Bear Creek*, issued by Herbert Jenkins, London, in an apparently very low print run. The book has become legendary as only seventeen copies are known to survive, seven of which institutionally held. Eight of the ten privately held copies are in (really) bad to average shape. One is in excellent shape but lacks the dustjacket, and the last one, formerly part of Glenn Lord's collection, and also in excellent condition, is the only known copy in the world with a dustjacket. Did you say rare?

7. Howard and his "old trusted typewriter"

Everyone "knows" that Howard typed his stories on an Underwood no. 5. Just like everyone "knows" Howard had typed a poem before committing suicide. But did he?

What we know for sure is that Howard had two typewriters. He acquired the first one in 1922 and kept it until early July 1925. The second one lasted him until his death. All the Conan, Solomon Kane and Kull stories were typed on the second machine. Although we know exactly when Howard bought the new typewriter, and the differences between the two machines are visible, he never mentions anywhere that he bought an Underwood, much less a number 5, nor does his father or any contemporary account. The oldest source we have for this comes from a remark made on April 1, 1965 by Jack

Scott—then the editor of the *Cross Plains Review*, the small town's weekly newspaper: "Howard had an old Underwood #5 typewriter. His last act before his suicide was to type a quotation from his poem with the line: 'The feast is over and the lamps expire.' Given what we now know about the suicide note, it could be that Howard never owned an Underwood no. 5 in the first place.

According to Glenn Lord, Howard's battered machine had been thrown away by his father a few weeks after his son's death. Supposing for an instant that Howard did own an Underwood no. 5 after all, it would be tempting to imagine that it had somehow escaped destruction. So, how could you possibly recognize Howard's Underwood out of the 3,885,000 that were manufactured? While it is impossible to give a definite answer, we do know that Howard bought his machine in 1925. And since all the machines had serial numbers, Howard's was necessarily below 200,000 (machine #207000 was manufactured in December 1925). Still an impressive number, but drastically down from nearly four million. Howard's own typewriter would be a priceless collectible, but a generic Underwood from the 1920s is worth about $20 to $50 on the secondary market. Perhaps less if in average or bad condition. Spend your money wisely if you find, or are offered one, from 1928 or 1932…

"I am King Turlogh of Bal-Sagoth and my kingdom is fading in the morning sky. And therein it is like all other empires in the world—dreams and ghosts and smoke."

– Turlogh O'Brien

Chapter Eight
The Adaptations

1. Howard on the Big Screen

To date, no Howard story has ever been turned into a movie.

2. Howard (almost) on the Big Screen

Over the years, there have been quite a number of cinematographic projects revolving around the works of Robert E. Howard, all abandoned at various degrees of completion. We will simply mention the most significant ones, without any attempt at chronology. The earliest one known dates back to 1968, when the owner of Lancer Books (who was then the publisher of the Conan stories) was contacted by a producer who was considering adapting the Conan tales for television. It soon turned out that this would be a cinematographic project, after all. It seems things never went beyond that stage, for reasons unknown.

Dark Agnes (Christophe Gans)

Mentioned by Gans himself in 2014. A script has been completed, written by Gans (and a writing partner). The *Brotherhood of Wolves* director always has three or four projects in the air, and this one is a definite possibility at this stage. *Dark Agnes* wouldn't literally adapt any of the stories, but the opening of the movie would be extremely faithful to Howard's first chapter, recounting how Agnes came to become Dark Agnes: in a somewhat improbable early sixteenth century France, a young peasant woman stabs the man her father was trying to force her to marry and she flees through the woods to live a dark life of adventure and betrayal. Gans has always been a Howard fan, and especially of Agnes. This is, simply put, one of the very few projects where a Howard character could come alive on the big screen instead of the travesties we have been used to or are expecting.

Red Nails (2006)

Announced in pomp and fanfare, this animated movie directed by Victor Dal Chele was supposed to adapt faithfully the last Conan story. Many high profiles actors were attached to the project to give their voices, notably Ron Perlman (Conan), Cree Summer (Valeria) and Mark Hamill (Tolkemec). Mike Kaluta and Mark Schultz, artists extraordinaires and Howard fans both, were involved in the art direction. However, the official website ran dry rather quickly and the project was buried without any explanation.

Queen of the Black Coast (Robert Rodriguez, circa 2003).

Know, oh Prince, that when the Wachowski brothers were briefly in charge of the Conan license, they asked Robert Rodriguez if he was interested to direct a Conan movie. Rodriguez, a Texan, is another longtime Howard fan, and wanted to adapt "Queen of the Black Coast." A script is rumored to exist. Here again, things didn't go very far.

Black Colossus (circa 2012)

One of the projects developed as a possible sequel to the 2011 Conan movie starring Jason Momoa. The idea was to adapt faithfully the Howard story, only adding at the beginning of the movie a naval battle. There was no naval battle after the shipwreck that was Nispel's movie, which was enough to sink all the prospective follow-ups, faithful to Howard or not.

Iron Shadows in the Moon (Thailand, 2015)

A supposedly ultra-faithful adaptation of the Conan story, this low-budget movie was completed, entered post-production but was never released. What few images made it to the Internet did not reassure the fans, and the reputation and shoddy practices of the producer killed the movie before it could be released.

3. Robert E. Howard Literally on the Big Screen

The Whole Wide World (1996)

This movie doesn't adapt a Howard story, but *One Who Walked Alone*, Novalyne Price Ellis' memoir of the two years when she and Howard dated. The movie was shot not too far from Cross Plains, Texas (where Howard lived), with its exquisite photography and stellar performances by its two leads: Vincent d'Onofrio (who *is* Howard, in that movie) and up-and-coming Renee Zellwegger, who was perfect as Novalyne Price. The movie didn't perform too well, sadly. A period piece that is definitely worth watching, even for non-Howard fans.

4. Howard on the Small Screen

"Pigeons from Hell" (1961)

Howard's horror story "Pigeons from Hell" was adapted for *Thriller*, an anthology series hosted by Boris Karloff. The episode lasts 30 minutes and first aired on 6 June 1961. It was directed by John Newland, and stars Brandon de Wilde and Crahan Denton. This was the first—and to date last—filmed adaptation of a Howard story. Given the time and budget, it holds up extremely well and the result is nothing short of successful. Unanimously hailed as one of the best episodes of this long-running series, it is quite faithful to Howard's story (except for the conclusion.)

A scene from the 1961 Thriller *episode "Pigeons from Hell."*

The project we would have loved to have seen:

"Tales from the Darkside." In the early 1980s, Kirby McCauley, agent for Stephen King, was involved in a project for a new television series to be called "Tales from the Darkside," an anthology of standalone adaptations of horror stories by well known authors. Karl Edward Wagner was involved in the project and would later explain that in the works were at least a story by Stephen King and two by Howard: adaptations of "The Cairn on the Headland" and of "The Horror from the Mound." Sam Peckinpah had been approached to direct. Unfortunately, the project never went far, and only Wagner's full script for "The Horror from the Mound" survives, dated 10 May 1984.

5. Movies with Original Scripts Featuring Characters Created by Howard

Conan the Barbarian (John Milius, 1982)

The movie which introduced Conan to millions of people, and which turned Arnold Schwarzenegger into a movie star. One of the most famous original scores ever, and justly so. Whatever one may think of this movie, it is impossible to deny its impact on the field of fantasy and on popular culture. Milius, an accomplished director, whose career includes some absolute masterpieces, signs here the fantasy movie against which any other similar project was judged until the release of Jackson's *Lord of the Rings* trilogy in the early 2000s, no less.

The film doesn't adapt any Howard story, though it borrows several scenes and situations: the name Valeria ("Red Nails"), her coming back from the dead to save Conan (Bêlit in "Queen of the Black Coast"), the climbing of the tower ("The Tower of the Elephant") and the crucifixion scene ("A Witch Shall be Born"). The story is pure Milius, though, betraying his political and philosophical leanings, diametrically opposed to those of Howard. An excellent movie in its own right, Milius' Conan is everything but Howard's. Whoever believes Conan could turn a wheel for minutes, let alone years, has never read a Howard story.

Conan the Destroyer (Richard Fleischer, 1984).

Second movie of what was supposed to be a trilogy, *Conan the Destroyer* had, on paper, a lot going for it, mostly because Richard Fleischer, the man who had directed *The Vikings* (1959) was at the helm. Roy Thomas, who had successfully adapted many Howard Conan tales for Marvel, was involved, though Gerry Conway, one of Marvel's worst comic-book writers ever, was also present, which was definitely not a good omen. The result is simply awful. Thomas was visibly not inspired and Conway was equal to himself. The movie is a long kitsch bore that has aged badly. Very. The commercial failure of that second opus signed the death warrant of the projected third one

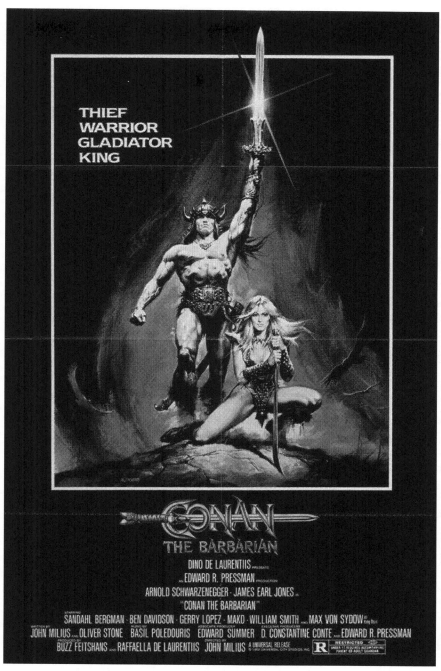

Conan the Barbarian *(1982) movie poster.*

Karl Edward Wagner, who had been hired to work on the script, had audacious ideas (as could be expected), but of course not a word of his would have ever reached the screen.

Solomon Kane (Michael Bassett, 2009)

Produced by Michael Berrow of Wandering Star, the movie had been optioned for many years. A few days before the option ran out, Berrow decided it was time to go for it and to resurrect this project, which had been essentially dormant since 1999, when a number of potential directors had been approached. Kane is played by James Purefoy, otherwise an excellent actor, but the character he plays has exactly one common point with the one created by Howard: his name. Unable to stop wallowing in self-pity, Purefoy keeps whining for two long hours while the rain insists on falling especially on him. A lost Balrog unexpectedly appears at the end to wake up the spectators. The movie was a flop in Europe and didn't even make it to the theaters in the States.

Conan (Marcus Nispel, 2011)

What to say about this trainwreck which showed definite promise on paper? A producer who openly stated he wanted to get back to the basics, an actor that was simply perfect for Conan (Jason Momoa was exactly the dark-skinned and pantherish character described by Howard). Interesting choices for the supporting characters (most notably Ron Perlman). Great initial ideas for the score (Tuomas Kantelinen (*Mongol*) was considered). And then a script that will be best described as dire, even after the script-doctor had worked his "magic." A third-rate director that did his meager best to ape Milius, a script riddled not with steel, but problems and holes, a score that is forgotten the second you come out of the theater, and the terrible decision to artificially turn the movie into a 3-D one, guaranteed to leave the spectator nauseous.

Kull the Conqueror (1997, John Nicolella)

Kevin Sorbo, Tia Carrere and Thomas Ian Griffith combine all their talents to try not to make us laugh. To no avail. Hailed as a turkey even before its release, it was as quickly forgotten as it had been made. To tuck snugly between your old VHS of *Hercules in New York* and *2020—Texas Gladiators*.

To be quite as thorough as possible, we should mention a few projects which never went beyond the initial stages, mercifully in the case of *Bran Mak Morn* (early 2000s, Wandering Star), in the initial script of which yet another astute producer had decided that Bran was actually the offspring of a Roman officer and a Pictish woman. Yes, some people are actually paid to come up with those ideas. A *Vultures of Wahpeton*, adapting Howard's best western was also considered at some point, with a scenario by Michael Tabb, as well as a project to bring the character of Thulsa Doom (Kull) to the big screen.

Other things best left forgotten…

Professionalism and exhaustiveness compel us to mention the TV series *Conan the Barbarian*, two seasons of an animated cartoon, as well as *Barbara the Barbarian*, a 1987 porn movie shot with infinitely more talent than Kevin Sorbo's *Kull*, and better acting than in the TV series (starring Kevin Sorbo).

6. Comic-Book Adaptations

"Crom the Barbarian" (1950, Avon)

Technically speaking, this is not an adaptation of the Conan stories, but a thinly disguised "homage" (i.e. without paying any rights). The first story, "Crom the Barbarian," appeared in *Out of this World* #1, published in June 1950. The story was written by Gardner F. Fox (who would later write his own heroic fantasy novels inspired by Howard), and drawn by John Giunta. Crom is a blond barbarian of the Æsir, roaming the world in a remote period of history. In the first

tale, he meets queen Tanit of Ophir. Crom would later return in *Strange Worlds* #1 (November 1950) and #2 (April 1951).
La Reina de la Costa Negra (Mexico, 1952-1966).

The history of this series published in Mexico is still full of holes, but it is there that Howard was first adapted in graphic format. The series began with issue 8 of a magazine titled *Cuentos de Abuelito* ("Grandpa's Stories"), adapting Howard's "Queen of the Black Coast" with two major changes, though: Conan became a blond warrior and Bêlit survives at the end of the story. A second series followed in 1958-1959, lasting at least eleven issues, perhaps sixteen, no one knows at the moment, so elusive are copies of that second series. A third and final run, lasting at least 53 issues, was published in 1965-1966, the early issues of which were reprints of the 1958-1959 series. The series ceased publication when L. Sprague de Camp sent a letter to the publisher. While a few issues have surfaced these last few years, all three series are rare to extremely rare. Only a handful of copies are known for most issues, and none at all for some of them.

"The Valley of the Worm" unpublished, and maybe never drawn 1959, Gil Kane.

In 1959, Gil Kane, the legendary artist of Green Lantern and Atom for DC Comics (then still called National), a future pioneer of the graphic novel format in the USA, and a true Howard aficionado, contacted Oscar J. Friend who was in charge of the Howard material and bought the rights to the James Allison story "The Valley of the Worm," starring James Allison. This would never come to be, but Roy Thomas and the same Gil Kane would eventually adapt the tale for Marvel Comics, where it was published in *Supernatural Thrillers* #3... in 1973, twenty-four years later.

Star-Studded Comics #14, (1968, Texas Trio)

"Gods of the North" was the first official adaptation of a Howard tale, "The Frost King's Daughter". The short story, starring Amra of Akbitana, was a slight rewrite of the Conan tale "The Frost Giant's Daughter," which had been rejected by *Weird Tales*. Larry Herndon wrote the script, Steven Kelez and "a host of others" drew it, Alan

The Mexican Conan comic La Reina de la Costa Negra.

Hutchinson inked it. The Texas Trio had a number of faithful followers, forming a loosely knit association, among whom were Glenn Lord, agent for the Howard heirs, and a young man who was in the habit of sending letters to his favorite Marvel Comics: George R. R. Martin.

Conan the Barbarian (1970, Marvel Comics, 275 issues + annuals and specials)

Roy Thomas, a former high school teacher who had left his position to work for Marvel in the mid-sixties and had soon become Stan Lee's closest assistant, wanted Marvel to expand its horizons. Jack Kirby had left the company for the competition, and the so-called "Silver Age" of comics was coming to an end. Thomas was looking for less traditional heroes, and he eventually managed to convince Martin Goodman, the publisher, to test the waters. A survey among the readers revealed that Conan was the character they wanted to see adapted.

Thomas thought the publishing phenomenon was out of his monetary reach, especially so since Goodman had given him a meager amount to spend. In desperation, Thomas approached Lin Carter, author of the abysmal Thongor books, heroic fantasy novels influenced by Howard and Edgar Rice Burroughs. When Carter's agent became too greedy, Thomas decided to give Conan a shot after all, and he got in touch with Glenn Lord. Embarrassed by the $150 per issue he could offer, Thomas told Lord they would pay $200, reflecting that, at the very worst, he would write the series himself and give his share back to Goodman. Goodman agreed to pay $200, but asked for a cheap artist to compensate the expense. Thomas' first choice, John Buscema, who had been Marvel's superstar after Jack Kirby's departure, was too expensive. Buscema was eager to draw Conan, as he had never liked to draw superheroes in the first place, but Thomas had to opt for a cheap Britisher, freshly arrived from England, and who had even drawn his first pages on a Manhattan bench: Barry Smith.

After a try-out story, the first issue of *Conan the Barbarian* appeared on the newsstands with an October 1970 cover date. Sales were good, but started sagging soon after, and it was decided to discontinue the magazine after a few issues. Thomas fought for the magazine, obtained a reprieve, and almost immediately, sales started to go up. In a matter of months, Conan became one of Marvel's most successful titles, commercially and critically speaking, winning an impressive number of awards. Barry Smith, who had begun his stint as a poor man's Jack Kirby, morphed into an accomplished artist in his own right and took every issue as a new challenge.

In 1971, Marvel launched a magazine titled *Savage Tales*. Unhampered by the Comics Code Authority (which didn't concern magazines), Thomas and Smith could give free rein to their imagination, adapting first "The Frost Giant's Daughter," then "Red Nails," still unequalled in their mastery and excellence 35 years later. Smith would grow disenchanted with the comics industry and leave after three exceptional years. His last issue on the comic book, "The Song of Red Sonja" (#24), was his swan song on the color series. Smith's Sonja has definite common points with Howard's Sonya, as portrayed in the historical tale "The Shadow of the Vulture." She was back soon after, this time sporting the "costume" she would become famous for (designed by artist Esteban Maroto): an improbable chainmail bikini. Red Sonja contests became a staple of mid-1970s comic conventions, and the character soon starred in her own comic-book series.

Gil Kane had drawn two fill-in issues during the Smith run, but the early days of Conan were now far behind, and the title had be-

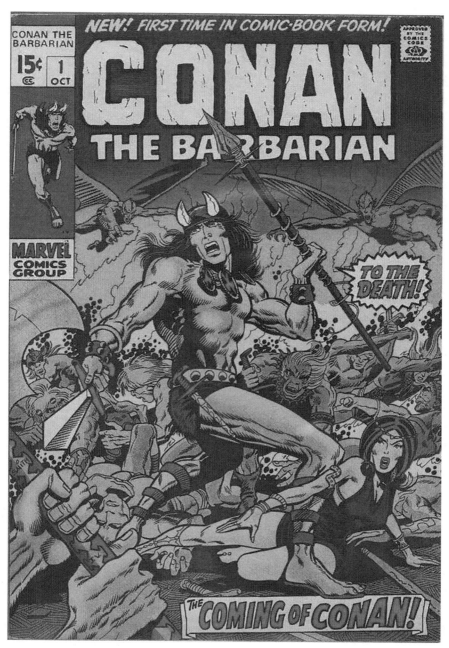

Conan the Barbarian *No. 1 (Marvel 1970)*

come so successful that hiring John Buscema to take over wasn't a problem anymore. It is doubtful even he could have imagined that he would draw thousands of pages over the years and that Conan would be the character he would come to be the most associated with. He was drawing him every month or so in *Conan the Barbarian* and in *The Savage Sword of Conan*, a magazine Marvel had launched in 1974. Buscema has become for many the quintessential comic-book Conan artist. The quality of his work depended a lot on the skills of the inker he was teamed with, and his association with artists such as Alfredo Alcala or Tom Palmer produced wonderful results.

Thomas left the series after ten years. It was obvious, reading the later issues, that he was losing interest, and understandably so. The title lingered for yet another ten years, best forgotten, before it was axed. The license was not renewed and the rights landed at Dark Horse, where the series was relaunched in a series of successful reboots, more modern in tone and style. Dark Horse also embarked on an ambitious series of reprints of the Marvel issues, albeit marred by garish coloring which ruin the experience. One of Marvel's best series of the early seventies, *Conan the Barbarian* is one of the rare major comic-book series which still hasn't been reprinted in a satisfying format.

7. Playing Conan

Here again, impossible to be exhaustive. We will concentrate on the more recent games, where the keyword is "fidelity to the source material."

Conan (tabletop boardgame, Monolith, 2016).

Launched in early 2015, the crowdfunding campaign that financed the game smashed all previous records. Conan became the best-funded boardgame in the history of Kickstarter. It took many years for the game to take off, but its conceptor, Fred Henry, wanted it to be the best possible game. Consequently, he hired experts and major players in their respective fields. This included a Howard expert to ensure the game would be true to its source, withing the limitations that are inherent to a boardgame. With 16,000 units pre-sold on Kickstarter, an additional 30,000 in production for retail sale, the Conan game—out in October 2016—is sure to be a major success. Immersion is a key aspect in tabletop gaming, and the new game is already sending a record number of people to their bookstores so they can become familiar with the actual stories.

Robert E. Howard's Conan: Adventures in an Age Undreamed of (RPG, Modiphius Games, 2017)

The Conan role-playing game. While the project had been in the works before the Monolith crowdfunding campaign, it was the success of the "back to the Howardian basics" policy of Monolith that convinced Modiphius their RPG should also be Howard-centric and to hire Howard scholars to ensure that. This was a second crowdfunding success for Conan. Monolith has clearly shown the way, and game developers are taking notice.

Tony Bath should be mentioned at some point. A Britisher and a fan of wargames taking place in Antiquity and the Middle Ages, Bath conceived and developed a series of rules for a wargame set in the Hyborian Age as early as 1956. *The Tony Bath Hyborian Campaign* was eventually published in 1962.

Age of Conan: Hyborian Adventures (video game, 2008, later: *Age of Conan: Unchained.*)

The Conan MMORPG (Massively Multiplayer Online Role Playing Game). The visuals of the game are striking, and quite Hyborian-like. You can play anyone you want… except Conan.

Chapter Nine
The Good, the Bad, and the Ugly

1. Howard and Tolkien: A Few Dates

Howard remains far, very far, behind Tolkien in terms of recognition and success, even if the Texan has been gaining ground since his works began to be published in respectful editions. The major works of the two pillars of modern fantasy share several points in terms of their publishing history: the first hardcover edition came out in the 1950s (1950 for *Conan the Conqueror*, 1952 for *The Lord of the Rings*) and the first paperback edition in the mid-1960s, with sales reportedly in excess of a million copies for both authors.

Tolkien was opposed to a cheap—paperback—edition of his magnum opus. Donald Wollheim, at Ace books, found what he thought was a legal loophole in Tolkien's rights for an American edition, and published *The Lord of the Rings* without permission from Tolkien in 1965, which became an overnight sensation. Tolkien had no choice but to counteract, and he thus arranged for an official, authorized, edition with Ballantine Books.

Three years earlier, in 1962, the same Don Wollheim had started to reprint the works of Edgar Rice Burroughs in popular editions. Sales were good, boosted notably by the superb covers of Roy Krenkel, soon helped, then replaced by his protégé: Frank Frazetta. Wollheim, who reprinted Howard's heroic fantasy novel *Almuric* in 1964, couldn't publish Conan since L. Sprague de Camp was already working on having the Cimmerian tales published. The deal to have the Conan stories published (edited by de Camp) was signed in September 1964 (a full year *before* the Ace Books edition of Tolkien). No sooner had the contract been signed that Martin Greenberg, owner of Gnome Press (which had published the Conan stories in hardcover in the 1950s) claimed he still had the rights to the stories, thus delaying publication until the matter was settled, which took over a year. The first Conan book—*Conan the Adventurer*, sporting a stunning Frank Frazetta cover—appeared in 1966, a year after Tolkien, but not because of him.

2. Howard and Frazetta.

If ever writer and artist were linked in the public's mind, it was indeed the duo Robert E. Howard and Frank Frazetta. Lancer Books, who had just obtained the rights to Conan, approached the artist responsible for the splendid covers illustrating the Burroughs reprints at Ace Books. Their offer was simple: while Frazetta was offered $200 per cover and they kept the art, Lancer proposed him $400 and they returned the artwork to him. Frazetta had always held on to his originals, and it was only his difficult financial situation in 1962 that had previously led him to accept to let the publisher keep his art (which was then of course sold behind his his back.) He read the Conan stories—though in later years he would claim he hadn't—and started painting. His Conan was, simply put, a pure expression of relentless savagery. Everything that had appeared before suddenly seemed sedate. Frazetta's Conan breathes menace, power, is vibrant with life, inordinately muscled, scarred, and definitely not someone you want to find on your way. Frazetta would later mention Charles Bronson and Jack Palance, two of Hollywood's most notorious B-movie mugs. His depiction of a long-haired Conan was not to the liking of editor L. Sprague de Camp, though.

Conan the Adventurer was published in 1966. Frazetta would later explain that the timing was just perfect, as the total freedom he was given and the subject matter were exactly what he needed at that particular time of his life. It was also very much in the spirit of the times. In a matter of months Conan became an icon, and Frazetta a star and America's most famous cover artist. His undisputed reign over American cover artists would last two decades, leaving far behind a host of more-or-less able imitators and wannabes. In the fifteen years that followed, about everything Howard had ever written would be published, and even printed in paperback. Buyers captivated by the sheer

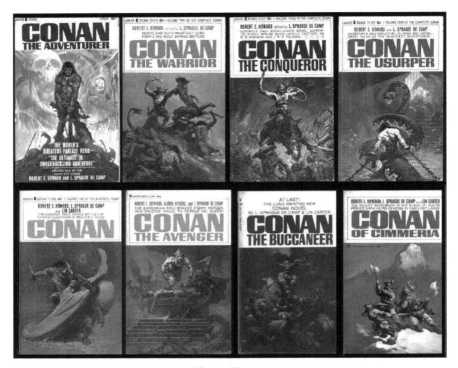

The Lancer Conan paperbacks with Frank Frazetta covers.

hypnotic force of Frazetta had also discovered that, for once, what the covers were promising, was indeed to be found inside.

In 2000, British publisher Wandering Star decided to reunite the tandem once more, for a volume titled *The Ultimate Triumph*: a compendium of Howard's best tales on the subject of barbarism as illustrated by Frank Frazetta. The artist was still struggling with the thyroid problems that had been plaguing him for years and he was unable to provide new illustrations. It was thus a Frazetta collector and specialist that went through the master's archives to select well over a hundred illustrations, most of which were previously unpublished, to be included in the lavish book.

While most of the Conan paintings are still with the Frazetta family, two have sold in the past few years, one in 2009 for a million dollars to Metallica guitarist Kirk Hammett, the second the following year for $1.5 million, to an anonymous buyer. Outrageous as these prices may appear, it seems the two buyers made a wise investment: a non-Conan painting, definitely not on a par with the iconic Conan images, recently sold for over a million dollars.

3. Did L. Sprague de Camp Save Conan (and Howard) from Oblivion?

L. Sprague de Camp had his eyes set on Conan ever soon after he discovered Howard in 1951. Smelling the potential of the series, he took over for his friend John D. Clark on the editorial duties for the Gnome Press volumes, which reprinted the stories originally published in *Weird Tales*. He then wormed his way in the writing process when three unpublished Conan stories were discovered in the files of Oscar Friend, who had succeeded Otis A. Kline at the head of the literary agency. While the three stories de Camp found were complete and in final form, he embarked on rewriting them, essentially by paraphrasing them. Next, he took some other unpublished Howard tales and turned them into Conan tales by adding a fantasy element.

It didn't take long before his actions were noticed, and he had to chomp at the bit—for a number of years. In 1964, when the dust had settled, or so he thought, de Camp repackaged the Conan stories, rewriting portions of some, completing the unfinished Howard tales, and added a large number of Conan stories he had authored himself to fill the so-called "gaps" Howard had left in what de Camp called the "saga." He then tried to shop the series around. By his own account, all the publishers he approached rejected the series until he found a home at Lancer Books, a rather small outfit whose publishing activities have long been rumored to be a front for money-laundering operations.

There is no reason to doubt de Camp when he states the series was turned down by so many publishers, but the real question is: why would they turn down such an opportunity, when everything showed fantasy was selling more and more? The answer had probably nothing to do with the potential of the series, but with the fact that the prospective publishers were also made to buy de Camp's stories in the package. To imagine for a second that Don Wollheim would have refused the opportunity to publish Conan is ludicrous: he had corresponded with Howard, had published him in fanzines in the 30s, had been the first to resurrect him in magazines in the 40s, had been the first to publish a Conan paperback (1953) and had just published *Almuric* in paperback (1964). Wollheim turning down Conan? The truth is that the Conan tales took a long time to get back in bookstores because de Camp shoehorned any potential publisher into using his own tales as well. In other words, de Camp was probably responsible for the *delay* it took to bring Howard back on the shelves. Howard was a talented writer, who didn't need the efforts of such a champion as de Camp. To imagine that the latter's editorial genius was required before Howard was reprinted is naïve. As early as 1962, Howard's return on the bookshelves was only a question of time, not of person.

4. With friends like these...

"There is one rather smart writer now who has been doing some work for us in rewriting several Howard stories, and he keeps pressing for a larger cut and keeps slipping in side remarks to the effect that if he wants to he can and will go ahead on his own and write about Conan as the author is dead, etc., etc. And I've warned him that I'll sue the pants off him if he makes one silly move of this nature before the Conan material runs out of copyright (56 years)."

> – Oscar J. Friend to the Howard rights owners, 14 March 1954. At that time, only one person had rewritten Howard stories: L. Sprague de Camp.

"Howard was maladjusted to the point of psychosis"

> – L. Sprague de Camp, introduction to *Conan*, Lancer Books, 1967.

"I think REH's personal psychological quirks contributed greatly to the emotional intensity of his stories—his paranoid delusions of persecution. That, I suspect, is one reason that some readers do not like Carter's and my Conan stories nearly so well as Howard's: we are not crazy the way he was, and hence we find his emotional intensity hard to imitate."

> – L. Sprague de Camp, interview, *REH: Lone Star Fictioneer* #4, 1976.

"My candid opinion of Howard's Conan v. those of his modern pasticheurs (myself included) is that, while some of the more recent stories are more smoothly done than REH's, with fewer inconsistencies and unlikely coincidences, none has quite the hypnotic intensity of Howard's originals. The reason is that none of us suffers from the fears, hatreds, and obsessions that bedeviled Howard. Obviously, I am not going to go to my neighborhood shrink and say, 'Hey, doc, will you please unbalance me so I can write as intensely as Robert Howard?'"

> – L. Sprague de Camp, letter to REHupa (Robert E. Howard United Press Association), 11 April 1984.

"If you asked me what, in my experience, was my biggest mistake in reviving and popularizing Conan, I should say that, while of course I should do some things differently, the biggest error was in picking Lin Carter as a collaborator instead of trying other possibilities first. I chose Carter because his natural style differed from REH's in one direction while mine differed in just the opposite; so I thought a collaboration might produce something close to the model.... Carter had many virtues and substantial talents, and was a very likable fellow, but such faults as cocksureness and irresponsibility largely nullified them. He never grew up."

> – L. Sprague de Camp, letter to REHupa, 26 January 1992.

"No, I wouldn't dream of censoring REHUPAns' reading matter. It's a case, not of censorship, but of simple, commercial, capitalistic greed, in the present political climate deemed one of the highest virtues. This led me to make a few tiny changes in REH's sacred text, so that I could sell the result and derive the maximum profit therefrom."

> – L. Sprague de Camp, letter to REHupa, 28 June 1995.

5. "A few tiny changes…"

So as to sell himself as a co-author of the Conan tales (a "post-humous collaborator", as he had it), de Camp had to show that his involvement was necessary. As it was difficult to bring changes to the stories as published in *Weird Tales*, de Camp had to work on the stories he found at the Friend agency: "The Frost Giant's Daughter," "The God in the Bowl," and "The Black Stranger". In case this was not clear, these three Howard stories were in final form and complete. A before and after should speak for itself (courtesy of Rusty Burke):

Howard's typescript:
"Heimdul roared and leaped, and his sword flashed in deathly arc. Conan staggered and his vision was filled with red sparks as the singing blade crashed on his helmet, shivering into bits of blue fire. But as he reeled he thrust with all the power of his broad shoulders behind the humming blade. The sharp point tore through brass scales and bones and heart, and the red-haired warrior died at Conan's feet."

Sprague de Camp version no. 1, *The Coming of Conan*, Gnome Press, 1953:
"Heimdul roared and leaped, his sword flashing in a deadly arc. At the same instant Conan thrust forward in a long lunge with all the power of his broad shoulders behind the blade. The Vana-heimer's singing blade crashed on Conan's helmet, staggering him and filling his vision with red sparks, but at the same instant his own sharp point tore through brass scales and bones and heart, and the red-haired warrior died at Conan's feet, the fragments of his sword, shivered into bits of blue fire, falling into the snow around him."

Sprague de Camp version no. 2, *Conan of Cimmeria*, Lancer Books, 1969:
"Heimdul roared and leaped, his sword flashing in a deadly arc. As the singing blade crashed on his helmet, shivering into bits of blue fire, Conan staggered, and his vision was filled with red sparks. But, as he reeled, he thrust with all the power of his broad shoulders behind the blade. The sharp point tore through brass scales and bones and heart, and the red-haired warrior died at Conan's feet.

Howard's typescript:

"Her maddening laughter floated back to him, and foam flew from the barbarian's lips. Further and further into the wastes she led him. The land changed; the wide plains gave way to low hills, marching upward in broken ranges. Far to the north he caught a glimpse of towering mountains, blue with the distance, or white with the eternal snows. Above these mountains shone the flaring rays of the borealis. They spread fan-wise into the sky, frosty blades of cold flaming light, changing in color, growing and brightening."

Sprague de Camp version no. 1, *The Coming of Conan*," Gnome Press, 1953:

"Foam flew from the barbarian's lips as her maddening laughter floated back to him. As the hours passed and the sun slid down its long slant, to the horizon, the wide plain gave way to low hills marching upward in broken ranges. As he panted up over the crests of the swells he glimpsed towering mountains farther north, their eternal snows blue with distance and pink in the rays of the blood-red setting sun. In the darkling sky above them shone the flaring rays of the aurora, spread fan-wise into the sky, frosty blades of cold flaming light, growing and brightening and changing in color, brighter than Conan had ever seen it."

Sprague de Camp version no. 2, *Conan of Cimmeria*, Lancer Books, 1969:

"Foam flew from the barbarian's lips as her maddening laughter floated back to him. Farther and farther into the wastes she led him. As the hours passed and the sun slid down its long slant to the horizon, the land changed ; the wide plains gave way to low hills marching upward in broken ranges. Far to the north he caught a glimpse of towering mountains, their eternal snows blue with distance and pink in the rays of the blood-red setting sun. In the darkening skies above them shone the flaring rays of the aurora. They spread fanwise into the sky—frosty blades of cold, flaming light, changing in color, growing and brightening."

6. Glenn Lord

Glenn Lord (1931-2011) was Howard's undisputed champion, keeping the flame burning at a time when no one cared. Lord discovered Howard when he bought *Skull-Face and Others* (Arkham House, 1946), and quickly developed an interest in the life and works of the Texas writer. Born in Louisiana, but living in the suburb of Houston, Lord wasn't that far away from Cross Plains.

A lover of poetry, he formed the idea of publishing a volume that would contain the entirety of Howard's poetical output. The project grew in size and ambition as he was constantly getting in touch with more people and discovering new material. *Always Comes Evening*, titled after one of Howard's best poems, was released in 1957 through a partnership with Arkham House in an edition of 636 copies. The slim volume contained 56 poems, supposedly Howard's entire output.

As Lord was learning more and more about Howard, he soon heard of the fabled "trunk," that is to say the four boxes full of typescripts that Howard's father had sent to E. H. Price in California in 1944. Another batch of typescripts had landed at the Otis Kline agency and was easier to locate, though many tales had gone missing over the years. It took Lord eight years between the moment he finally located the "trunk" in California and the day he received the last pages. He had to offer money in the end to help smoothe the process. In the early seventies, Lord was now in possession of over fifteen thousand pages of Howard typescripts and documents that would prove of inestimable value for the fans, the readers and the scholars.

In 1965, de Camp was offered to become the agent for the Howard heirs, a position he declined, recommending Lord instead. He probably thought the man would be easy to maneuver, but learned the hard way he had been very wrong. Lord accepted the offer and took his job very seriously. In 1961, he had launched *The Howard Collector*, his Howard fanzine, and had been learning a few things about the publishing world in the process. He knew how to deal with large paperback firms, specialty publishers, and fans. Thanks to his tireless efforts, Howard was soon present everywhere, from fanzines to classy semi-professional booklets, from hardcovers with limited print-runs to mass-market paperbacks. By the mid-seventies, virtually every story Howard had penned was available in one form or another, a mere ten years after Lord had become the agent for the rights-holders.

Lord was instrumental in having the pure-text Berkley editions of Conan stories published in the 1970s under the editorship of Karl Edward Wagner. Years later, when he was no longer agent, he furnished the Wandering Star crew all the material they needed for the books, and continued to do so even though there was some very bad blood between him and the then rights-holders. Lord's collection, probably representing over 95 percent of the surviving Howard documents and typescripts, is now housed at the Harry Ransom Center in Austin, Texas.

Glenn Lord passed away on December 31, 2011.

"I got a long letter from Lovecraft. That boy is plenty smart. And well read too. He starts out by saying that most of my arguments seem logical enough and that he is about on the point of accepting my views—and then follows with about three or four closely written pages with which he rips practically all my theories to shreds. He's out of my class. I'm game to go the limit with a man my weight, but me scrapping with him is like a palooka climbing into the ring with a champion.

— Robert E. Howard, July 1930.

Chapter Ten
Dear Mr. Lovecraft...

(Selected paragraphs from the letters sent by Howard to H.P. Love-craft)

"I simply believe in the fundamental equality of men; I recognize the fact that certain men will always be shrewder, or stronger, or braver, or more intelligent than others. But if anybody has any rights, everybody has those rights." (circa September 1933)

"Barbaric life was hell; but so is modern life." (circa September 1933)

"My antipathy for Rome is one of those things I can't explain myself. Certainly it isn't based on any early reading, because some of that consisted of MacCauley's *Lays of Ancient Rome* from which flag-waving lines I should have drawn some Roman patriotism, it seems. At an early age I memorized most of those verses, but in reciting, changed them to suit myself and substituted Celtic names for the Roman ones, and changed the settings from Italy to the British Isles! Always, when I've dreamed of Rome, or subconsciously thought of the empire, it has seemed to me like a symbol of slavery—an iron spider, spreading webs of steel all over the world to choke the rivers with dams, fell the forests, strangle the plains with white roads and drive the free people into cage-like houses and towns." (circa February 1931)

"I have no idyllic view of barbarism—as near as I can learn it's a grim, bloody, ferocious and loveless condition. I have no patience with the depiction of the barbarian of any race as a stately, god-like child of Nature, endowed with strange wisdom and speaking in measured and sonorous phrases." (circa November 1932)

186

"In the case of the oppression of people by a ruling class, or classes, it is quite true that the revolutions of Russia and France show that tyrannies ultimately fall; however each overthrow was preceded by many centuries of oppression, in which generation after generation groaned under the crushing heel, before the change came about. Change apparently being one of the laws of Nature, we can not expect despotisms to endure indefinitely any more than republics, democracies, or periods of chaotic anarchy. I do not expect a permanent state of slavery, but I do look for a period of more or less length, in which class and individual liberty will be practically unknown—oh, it won't be called slavery or serfdom. They'll have another name for it—Communism, or Fascism, or Nationalism, or some other -ism; but under the surface it will be the same old tyranny, modified, no doubt, to fit modern conditions. The victims probably won't realize they are slaves for a long time, until conditions get too utterly hellish. (circa December 1932)

"You accuse me of 'hating human development' because I mistrust Fascism. Well, there can't be much tolerance about a system whose advocates denounce as "enemies of humanity" anyone who disagrees with them…. Of course you can draw glowing pictures of a Fascist Utopia. But you can not prove that Fascism is anything but a sordid, retrogressive despotism, which crushes the individual liberty and strangles the intellectual life of every country it inflicts with its slimy presence. The Fascist movement in this country is nothing new; it is merely presented under a new name; it is the same old gang that in bygone days were called Tories, or Federalists, or Black-Republicans, or Hoover-Republicans—the same gang that are now hamstringing the administration and yelling 'Communism!' every time Roosevelt tries to free the country a little from their monopolistic clutch. I know it is the fad now to sneer at Democracy; but Democracy is not to blame for the troubles of the world. The men who are most to blame are the very men who now would 'save' the country under the new name of Nazis, or Fascists…. Of course, you say that the type of Fascism you advocate is without despotism and persecution of intellectual freedom; you might as well say you advocate a cobra without its venom, a skunk without its stench, or a leper without his scabs." (circa December 1934)

"I am unable to identify myself with any definite class or political movement.... If it came to a show-down, I suppose it would be natural for me to throw in with the working classes, since I am a member of that class, but I am far from idealizing—or idolizing—it or its members. In the last analysis, I reckon, I have but a single conviction or ideal, or whatever the hell it might be called: individual liberty. It's the only thing that matters a damn. I'd rather be a naked savage, shivering, starving, freezing, hunted by wild beasts and enemies, but free to go and come, with the range of the earth to roam, than the fattest, richest, most bedecked slave in a golden palace with the crystal fountains, silken divans, and ivory-bosomed dancing girls of Haroun al Raschid. With that nameless black man I could say:

> "Freedom, freedom,
> Freedom over me! –
> And before I'd be a slave,
> I'd like down in my grave
> And go up to my God and be free!"
> (circa December 1932)

Chapter Eleven

Reading about Howard

Books

One Who Walked Alone (Novalyne Price Ellis, Donald M. Grant, 1986)

If you can read only one book to understand Bob Howard the man, Novalyne Price's book is this book. She grew up near Brownwood and became friends with Tevis Clyde Smith, one of Howard's best friends, in high school. In 1933, the young woman, who had literary aspirations, was introduced to Bob Howard. A year later, Novalyne accepted a teaching position at the Cross Plains high school and renewed her acquaintance with Howard. Very soon, they were dating. Novalyne kept a diary (she thought the practice would help her with her writing) and preserved it. Fifty years later, irritated by the portrayal of Howard made by the de Camps, she decided it was time to publish her side of the story. The book offers a fascinating, if personal, window on Bob Howard the man, who literally comes alive in these pages. Covering Howard's last two years, this book is, simply put, indispensable.

The Dark Barbarian (Don Herron (Ed.), Greenwood Press, 1984)

Conceived and edited by Don Herron, *The Dark Barbarian* was a landmark in Howard criticism. Openly hostile to L. Sprague de Camp, Herron took his subject matter seriously, focusing not on Conan, but on Howard as a gifted and important author. Most of the essays are now seriously dated, given the enormous amount of new information that has come to light since it appeared, but that doesn't diminish the historical importance of the volume. "Robert E. Howard: Hard-Boiled Heroic Fantasist" by George Knight (an alias for Don Herron), is perhaps the single most important essay about Howard ever published, burying in ten pages everything that had been written before about the influences of Howard and delineating his true importance in the landscape of American genre fiction. A follow up of sorts, *The Barbaric Triumph* (2004), is a far cry from that pioneer effort.

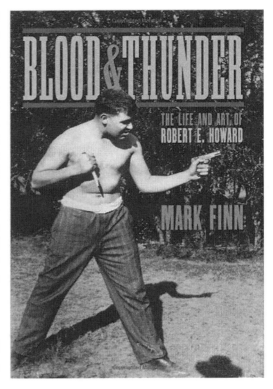

Blood and Thunder by Mark Finn, 2010 revised edition.

The Last Celt (Glenn Lord (Ed.), Donald M. Grant, 1976)

Glenn Lord's monumental bio-bibliography. In the age of the Internet, bibliographies have become a thing of the past, but Lord's impressive mass of essays, memoirs, documents, rarities and reproductions remains a beautiful production and a monument to Howard, written and supervised by the man who was Howard's greatest champion.

Dark Valley Destiny (Catherine and L. Sprague de Camp, Jane Whittington Griffin, Bluejay Books, 1983)

The first full-length biography of Howard. We could be polite and say that this book suffers from a series of errors, approximations and peremptory judgments. But that would be too kind. The de Camps have taken liberties with their evidence, hiding certain aspects, twisting others, and inventing facts when they couldn't find any to back up their theories. Nothing in this book should be taken at face value unless checked against other sources. While the de Camps must be lauded for interviewing so many people before they passed away, all their research material has now been made available to scholars, and their biography can now be relegated where it belongs: in the footnotes of the history of Howard scholarship.

Blood and Thunder, the Life and Art of Robert E. Howard (Mark Finn, 2006, 2010)

The first edition of this book (2006, MonkeyBrain Books) has now been replaced with its updated and expanded version (2010, REH Foundation Press). Finn, a native Texan, offers here a biography of Howard as seen and examined through the prism of Texas. It's effective, often pertinent, and definitely necessary for a non-Texan. Finn, by his own admission, never had any intention of authoring a "definitive" biography, and he has often stated his book is there to bury *Dark Valley Destiny*, and help readers wait for the next mammoth-sized biography. The one biography to read until then.

Magazines

Cromlech

With three issues published in the 1980s, this was the first attempt at issuing a serious magazine about Howard. It was the brainchild of Marc Cerasini and Charles Hoffman, the latter having the honor to have been the author of the very first serious piece of writing about Howard ever: "Conan the Existentialist" (1974).

The Dark Man: the Journal of Robert E. Howard Studies

Published more or less regularly since 1990. The "academic" journal about Howard and his works. Plenty of excellent essays. Plenty others of dubious quality, too, in spite of permanent efforts to meet academic standards.

The Cimmerian

Leo Grin's prozine, had, during the six years of its existence, an impressive publication rhythm (between 6 and 12 issues a year), an avowed anti-academic stance and essays that ran from the excellent to the abysmal and/or fillers. Always looking for controversy and wishing to engage in polemics, *The Cimmerian* was a fiery comet in the Howardian landscape.

REH: Two-Gun Raconteur

Published since 1976 by the tireless Damon Sasser, TGR offers a successful cocktail of light and serious essays, illustrations, and rare Howard fiction.

The Robert E. Howard Days event (or Howard Days for short) take place every year on the second weekend of June in Cross Plains, Texas, Howard's hometown. It's an occasion for scholars, fans, amateurs and newbies to gather in the heart of Texas and discuss Howard where he wrote all the stories he is famous for. The theme and guest of honor change every year, and the Robert E. Howard Foundation Awards are announced.

Howard on the Internet:

Selected Websites:

The Robert E. Howard Foundation (www.rehfoundation.org/)

The official organ of the non-profit Foundation "organized to foster understanding of the life and works of Robert E. Howard. Its goal is to honor Howard's legacy as a skillful, prolific and successful writer of fantasy, regional, horror, action and adventure stories in a wide variety of genres. The mission of the Foundation is to promote its belief in the importance of imagination and creative writing." Different membership options possible, including a free level.

Robert E. Howard Days (www.howarddays.com/)

The official website of the annual Howard Days, held on the second weekend of June, in Cross Plains, Robert E. Howard's Texas hometown.

HowardWorks (http://howardworks.com/)

Far and wide, the most complete bibliographic database on Howard, period.

"Death to the old is inevitable, and yet somehow I often feel that it is a greater tragedy than death to the young. When a man dies young he misses much suffering, but the old have only life as a possession and somehow to me the tearing of a pitiful remnant from weak old fingers is more tragic than the looting of a life in its full rich prime. I don't want to live to be old. I want to die when my time comes, quickly and suddenly, in the full tide of my strength and health."

— Robert E. Howard, 9 May 1936

Conclusion

The Howard Revolution

Though Howard is often hailed as a Founding Father of modern Fantasy, the exact nature of what he brought to the genre is often misunderstood. For some, the creation of Conan the Cimmerian marks the birth of a new literary genre, "sword and sorcery," understood as an offspring of the (pseudo-)medieval romances of William Morris or E.R. Eddison, and characterized by the presence of a muscular hero, a non-Manichean intrigue, and a healthy dose of violence (on top of the "required" ingredients that are the swords and the sorcery). Needless to say, such a label is not really helpful. The very appellation has been used to denigrate the (sub)genre as a whole, in a nebulous equation that puts all novels belonging to this category at the same level, hence guilty of a lack of sophistication, an absence of literary value and an overt tendency for misogyny. If *that* defines Howard's contribution to literature, then there's no reason to be ecstatic. But, and as is often the case with the Texan, things are more complex than they appear.

Howard never uses the appellation "Conan the Barbarian" in the tales featuring the character. He introduces him as "the Cimmerian" or "of Cimmeria." In the same manner, his name is never featured in any of the titles in the series. He is sometimes a secondary character of sorts, notably in "The Black Stranger" or "A Witch Shall be Born." He is of course pivotal to the story, but acts mostly off-stage. In "Wolves Beyond the Border," he wasn't intended to be the focus of the story. Those three tales were written late in the series, proof that Howard was trying to break new grounds and not relying on a successful same-old formula. This phenomenon is in no way confined to Conan: Howard was fond of using recurring heroes in his tales, but it cannot be said that the stories revolve around them. They may act and behave similarly or differently from one story to another, but at no moment can we state that there is an evolution to the character. The stories are autonomous, do not feature any recurring character (aside from a few isolated examples), the protagonist doesn't have any destiny or quest to fulfill, and it is a futile attempt to try to chain him in a so-called biography. That "Queen of the Black Coast" takes place before or after "Black Colossus" doesn't affect the reader's experience in any way, whichever he thinks comes first in the "biography."

It was during the sixties, when the Conan series was first printed in paperback, that Conan suddenly found himself turned into the hero of eight volumes at first, then twelve, of a "saga" relating his slow ascension to the throne of Aquilonia, following a series of editorial rewritings and tinkerings that have been detailed at length elsewhere. To give but one example of this very damaging process at work: to reveal from the very beginning that the character appearing in the first chapter of "The Black Stranger" is Conan is a particularly unfortunate attempt at artificially recentering the narrative on the Cimmerian, while Howard was obviously avoiding to identify him as such and playing with the codes he had himself created, so as to make his own hero "disappear" throughout most of the tale.

The fetishisation of the name "Conan" has had numerous consequences, which are not without having a considerable influence on the way Howard's writings are perceived. Turning the character into a "franchise" has contributed to freeze, so to speak, certain aspects of the brand that the Cimmerian has become. One could of course object that these deformations are inevitable when a fictional character becomes such an icon, escaping its creator and taking on a life of its own. Furthermore, Howard himself wrote some not very commendable Conan tales when money was tight. However, Lovecraft is remembered and celebrated for "The Colour out of Space" and "The Call of Cthulhu", not "Horror at Red Hook." Yes, Howard did pen "The Vale of Lost Women", but just like any writer, he should be judged by his best production, not his worst. Howard is, first and foremost, the author of "Pigeons from Hell," "Red Nails," "Beyond the Black River," and "Worms of the Earth" (to name a few), stories dealing with decaying civilizations, death, savagery, isolation and madness. In those stories, most secondary characters meet their end and most of the time the protagonist barely survives the ordeal; decidedly not your typical escapist fare.

Conan's fame (and the deformations that accompany it perforce) came *before* Howard received any serious critical attention. By way of consequence, the literary quality of the stories has more often than not been only a secondary concern, behind the imposing and towering figure of Conan. Thus, if Tolkien is always referred to as the author of *The Lords of the Rings*, Howard is, at best, the "creator of Conan the Barbarian," never "the author of 'Red Nails.'"

The expression "sword and sorcery" was coined in 1961 by Fritz Leiber (author the Fafhrd and Gray Mouser stories) to describe the kind of stories Howard, Moorcock and himself wrote. Moorcock had suggested "epic fantasy." Not openly stated, but clearly important in the process was Moorcock's wish to give a name to a kind of fantasy that was different from Tolkien's. The problem is that Howard himself never put such a label on his writings, and probably never felt the need to. To him, his tales were "yarns" and when a story was written with *Weird Tales* in mind, it would be a "weird," with no more precision. He was not one to let himself be caged in the very narrow frame(s) imposed by the very nature of the pulp market. This attitude was instrumental in the inception of the Conan series and explains why quite a number of his tales were rejected, too audacious or groundbreaking for the era. This, in turn, explains part of Howard's genius, who recognized this problem and found a way to transcend those limitations.

Howard would probably have refused this compelling need to catalogue his works in such narrow confines, especially one as reductive as "sword and sorcery" (which sounds like a bad attempt at trying to describe by its trappings what one can't define). More: when the shelves of American bookstores began to be filled with an endless stream of sword and sorcery paperback novels in the mid-sixties, the avalanche was such that it led to a very logical counter-reaction, and the creation of yet a new appellation: "high fantasy." The other side of the spectrum thus became "low fantasy," implicitly rejected as a bastard and decidedly unsavory subgenre peopled with low-browed, fur-diapered, sword-wielding barbarian simpletons with a definite penchant for semi-naked bimbos. Those novels were most of the time the product of the limited talents and imagination of hacks eager to meet the then-huge editorial demand for such novels, and one can understand why several authors felt the need to distance themselves from this glut of bad fiction. (Karl Edward Wagner's "Appearing Soon at a Newsstand Near You" (*Fantasy Newsletter*, March 1981) is a must-read article in that respect, a radiography of the market as hilarious as it is frightening.)

Having "fathered" the sword and sorcery subgenre, Howard was soon enough lumped in with the rest of that crowd, often condemned for what he had written, and even more often for what people thought he had written. The frankly embarrassing novels authored by Lin Carter—himself responsible for several Conan pastiches—didn't help at all with the general confusion as to what was genuine Howard and what had been written by people cashing in on his name.

Howard never had any intention to tell us the long saga of a barbarian slowly rising up the rungs of a society of a distant past, he wasn't there to pen a national epic in the manner of the old legends. His fiction is anchored in realism (despite all its concessions to the supernatural), in his experience of life, as seen and filtered through the Great Depression. Conan's world is not "imaginary," for that matter, since the Hyborian Age is supposedly a forgotten era of our own History. The distinction is a capital one. Secondary as it may be, Howard's world is our own. Howard never tries to amaze us with wondrous animals or creatures. His bestiary is ours and the animal threats are those of our world, simply bigger: giant hyenas, enormous snakes, carnivorous gorillas, and even an elephant. The foes are almost always anthropomorphic: sorcerers that bleed, lust, age and die. The gods, if they exist, never interfere with human affairs, or if they do, by way of their human agents, we are free to believe those agents are divinely inspired or simply deranged.

Howard developed Conan's world the same way he had experienced with new genres: by hybridization. When he decided to write a vampire tale, he rejected the usual conventions of the genre, and changed the background to Texas, a place he knew and could write convincingly about; the Victorian protagonist was replaced with a decidedly obtuse and somewhat racist tenant farmer. By the same token, the Hyborian Age was born out of Howard's difficulty to sell historical fiction. He thus slightly modified the names of peoples and countries, lumped together his favorite historical and regional eras and created for himself a giant fictional playground where he was free to violate every historical detail without risking the irate reactions of readers appalled at his treatment of history, vampires or accepted conventions. For this was nothing new for him: as early as 1928, when he had first created Solomon Kane, the editor at *Argosy* had told Howard what one could do and couldn't do in fiction. Howard couldn't care less: he was a trendsetter by nature, not a follower.

He was in many ways the successor to the swashbucklers, those fast-moving, historical or epic adventures that were so popular in the early years of the twentieth century. He was an admirer of Alexandre Dumas, Harold Lamb and Rafael Sabatini, who almost define the genre by themselves. But by freeing himself from the contingencies and requirements of historical and even adventure fiction, Howard shattered all the boundaries that perforce limited his predecessors. He arrived on the literary scene precisely at the moment when it was no longer really possible to write about unexplored areas of the world. The Conan tales transcend by their very nature the genres they are derived from—be it western, history or high-adventure—by displacing them from their historical context and cloaking them in a Hyborian guise, Howard gave those stories a universality they would not have had otherwise. They became timeless, as truthful today as they were seventy years ago. And Howard went one step further, by liberating his hero from the yoke of (royal) destiny and/or biography that has proven such a quagmire for so many of his followers. With Howard, fantasy simply became Proteus-like in essence, the perfect vehicle to tell any kind of story one wants. Sadly, few were those that recognized this incredible breakthrough for what it was.

Beyond its pulpish excesses, Howard's fiction is characterized by its violence, by a certain cold lucidity on what mankind is capable of; it is brutally pessimistic (and thus prophetic) on many points, which is probably why it has always been at its most popular in times of crises, espousing the fault lines of our society: the 1930s, the second half of the sixties, and of course our present world. Howard did away with the *thous* and *thees*, the romantic overtones and the conviction that good necessarily prevails in the end, elements that are so prevalent in classic fantasy. He tells us about a world that is dark, dirty and gritty, where one may temporarily find refuge in the mad illusion that is adventure, but a world which offers, in the final analysis, not much in the way of hope. Howard tells us about the world we live in.

With his best tales, and notably the best Conan tales, Howard gives us an opus that is universal in scope, as modern today as it was in the 1930s. Perhaps even more modern.

About the Author

Patrice Louinet is the editor of the definitive, three-volume, Conan series (Del Rey Books). On the board of directors of the Robert E. Howard Foundation since its inception in 2006, he has edited numerous Howard books, as well as essays and introductions, and has acted as the Howard adviser on the immensely successful Conan boardgame from Monolith. He received the Lifetime Achievement Award from the Robert E. Howard Foundation in 2014 and was twice nominated for the Grand Prix de l'Imaginaire. He is presently completing his PhD dissertation on Howard at La Sorbonne, Paris (American Literature and Civilization Department), among other endeavors. Patrice lives in Paris, France, with his wife and son.

Made in the USA
Middletown, DE
06 March 2019